# Judaism

# Judaism

## A Way of Being

DAVID HILLEL GELERNTER

Yale University Press   New Haven and London

Set in Minion type by Integrated Publishing Solutions,
Grand Rapids, Michigan.
Printed in the United States of America by Sheridan Books,
Ann Arbor, Michigan.

Library of Congress Cataloging-in-Publication Data
Gelernter, David Hillel.
Judaism : a way of being / David Hillel Gelernter.
        p.      cm.
Includes bibliographical references and index.
ISBN 978-0-300-15192-3 (hardcover: alk. paper)
1. Judaism.   I. Title.
BM562.G45 2009
296—dc22
2009020159

Color plates (between pages 82 and 83): All paintings are by the
author, in acrylics and mixed media on panel (except for Ein Sof,
which is on paper). Photos by Ken Lovell of the Yale Digital Media
Center for the Arts, except for Shma, Echad, and Nariah,
by David Ottenstein of Ottenstein Photography.

A catalogue record for this book is available from
the British Library.

This paper meets the requirements of ANSI/NISO Z39.48–1992
(Permanence of Paper).

10 9 8 7 6 5 4 3

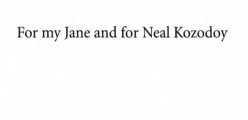

For my Jane and for Neal Kozodoy

# Contents

# Preface

This is a book about Judaism, but I believe you'll find it unlike any other book on Judaism you've ever read or are likely to read.

It is not a book about Jewish history, although history crops up frequently in the discussion.

It is not a book about Jewish religious practices or holidays, or the Jewish life cycle—although many prayers and practices and holidays are important to the argument.

It is not a book about Jewish teachings or religious doctrine, although it is full of Jewish teachings, including many that have become the common property of mankind—and many others that, although they are equally important, are virtually unknown to the world at large.

This is a book that answers, from the standpoint of normative, or "Orthodox," Judaism, the great questions of human existence:

1. How do we understand our place in the unspeakable vastness of creation, and our urge to encompass and comprehend all this vastness within the microminuscule specks of our own human minds?

2. Is physical creation all there is, or is there something beyond that gives it meaning, and requires us to grasp not only matter and energy but justice and injustice, truth and falsehood, good and evil? And can this "something" (also known as *God*) be known? Approached?

3. How do I order my life as a human being, as a sexual being, as one part of a family?

4. Does life have a goal beyond comfort, power, prosperity, survival? Is the goal salvation? Redemption? Are we on our own, or can we look to God for help, intervention, a guiding hand?

These questions sound philosophical, and they can't be discussed unless we dip into philosophy now and then. But here is the unusual (or strange) thing about this book: these four questions and their answers will present themselves not as philosophical propositions but as themes that resonate throughout a lived Jewish life, like melodies traveling up and down and all around an orchestra (from the violins to flutes to oboes to brass) over the course of a symphony. These themes are presented in this book just as they present themselves to practicing Jews: visually; as mental images. Observant Jews, as they concentrate on each detail of Jewish life, aren't necessarily aware of these images coalescing into themes, and the themes coalescing into the richly reverberant, soaring architecture of Judaism. (A pianist caught up in the beauty—or technical difficulty—of some phrase might not have the larger theme in mind, or the architecture of the composition as a whole, which is created by separate themes just as the themes are created by separate phrases and the phrases by separate notes.) But any observant Jew will recognize my image-themes; and I hope these ideas will seem natural to many non-observant Jews and non-Jews too.

In the first chapter I spell out the role of images and image-themes in Judaism, give some examples and formulate some hypotheses. The next four chapters correspond to the four questions above; in each case, Judaism's answer takes the form of a multilayered image. After summarizing the results, the last chapter makes several assertions about the unique beauty and truth of the Jewish worldview. Finally, three appendices deal with important issues that have arisen along the way but are not strictly central to the discussion.

This is a book for Jews who are unsatisfied with the usual approaches to the "message" of Judaism; who seek a firmer grasp of Judaism's point or purpose or reason-for-being. Such readers deserve the best—Judaism at full strength, straight up; no water, no soda, aged in oak for three thousand years. My standard in this book is accordingly what is called Orthodox Judaism. (Hasidism, as practiced by groups such as Chabad and many others, is a version or dialect of Orthodox Judaism. Many Orthodox Jews are not Hasidim, and "modern Orthodoxy," not Hasidism, is the most intellectually vigorous part of Orthodoxy today.) I do not assume, however, that readers will have any prior knowledge of Judaism or Jewish practice. Everything is spelled out; there are no prerequisites. In fact, since Judaism is not only the oldest but (paradoxically) the least known of the world's great religions, I assume that it must be introduced not just to Jews but to everyone.

A word about my own Jewish background. Although this book amounts in many ways to an explanation of Orthodoxy, my own viewpoint, for the record, is more complicated than might first appear. I grew up in a Reform community. (Reform is the branch that is furthest from Orthodoxy.) The grandfather who taught me Torah was an ordained Reform rabbi. He had been brought up strictly Orthodox, and over the years he'd had many disagreements with Reform Judaism. His personal practices as an adult remained essentially though not entirely Orthodox. But he was the devoted (and beloved) leader of a large Reform congregation, and he introduced me to Reform as well as Orthodox literature and ritual. I have many arguments with the non-Orthodox denominations myself, but cannot think of Reform Judaism or any other non-Orthodox branch without respect and affection.

I can best describe the goals of this book by borrowing a term invented by Israeli scholars: it is an attempt to lay out a "common Judaism," a Judaism whose beauties and animating principles can be recognized and (with qualifications) agreed to by all.

# Acknowledgments

The research that produced this book was sponsored and supported by the Shalem Center in Jerusalem. I'll always be grateful to Shalem and especially to Dan Polisar for their help and support at a critical time. I want to thank Yale University Press, especially Sarah Miller and Jeffrey Schier, for their expertise and their patience, and Jonathan Brent, for getting this ball rolling.

Mem Bernstein and Arthur Fried supported this work at the earliest stages, during the publication of a series of *Commentary* pieces. They are among the most disinterested and remarkable philanthropists I have ever met, happy to do vast amounts of good and stay strictly in the background. I have profited enormously from their generosity and kindness.

Roger Hertog's support and encouragement is in a class by itself. Roger is a famous philanthropist who has done enormous good to the American Jewish community and Jewish education, to research and education in Israel, and to many good causes unconnected with Jews and Judaism. But Roger is generous not only with (mere) money but with his energy, interest, encouragement, sympathy, wisdom, and (above all) his invaluable friendship.

Which brings me to Neal Kozodoy, who conceived this project on the basis of some of the author's scattered ideas, edited with brilliant and meticulous care a series of five *Commentary* pieces (arguing over, clarifying, distilling, and strengthening each idea and each sentence along the way), and then served as editor of this book with the same extraordinary, long-suffering devotion. He edited and improved an endless string of drafts and redrafts and new, improved redrafts, supported with his wisdom and generosity every aspect of the book-writing process; helped and guided the author every last step of the way. This book is inconceivable without him, and any good it does is Neal's doing. *Pirkei Avos* tells us, "Get yourself a teacher; find yourself a friend." In Neal I can say, with gratitude far beyond what I can ever express, that I found both.

And so I arrive finally at my grandfather, Rabbi Theodore N. Lewis, *zeicher tsaddik li'vracha.* He taught me Torah, and he was a luminous survivor of an earlier age: his sense of humor was fine, but he was wholly free of the corrupting irony that sticks to us nowadays like a sinister stray dog we can't shake. When he spoke of his love of Jews and Judaism, and of his family, he held nothing back. This incandescent love made him unforgettable to nearly everyone who ever met him. He was one of *hachmei ha'Mesorah,* the sages of our tradition. Looking in the small *Tanach* he always had with him I find (Isaiah 59:21), "My spirit which is upon you, and the words I gave you, shall not depart from your speech, or the speech of your descendants, or the speech of *their* descendants—says the Lord—henceforth and forever." And in the *siddur* from which he used to *daven* every day, I find his favorite quotation (*Avos* 1:12)—"Be one of Aaron's disciples, *oheiv shalom v'rodeif shalom,* loving peace and pursuing peace; *oheiv et ha'briot u'm'karvan la'Torah,* loving all creation and drawing it close to Torah."

# I
# Picturing Judaism

What is it about Judaism that is transfixing enough to have kept a brilliant, fractious, bickering, relentlessly skeptical people alive for three thousand years, made them the senior nation of the Western world, and turned them into a marvel and (too often) an obsession to so many of their fellow human beings?

Answering that question is the goal of this book. But first we American Jews must face reality. Judaism may be transfixing, but the numbers speak for themselves: America's Jewish community is shrinking relentlessly. It is melting like old snow into warm American earth. Except for Orthodox Jews, who are the most passionate but smallest part of the community, American Judaism might well be gone (or almost gone) within a generation or two.

*Why?* Why do so few American Jews feel close to Judaism? Why do so few teach it to their children, study the Bible or the rabbinic classics, go to synagogue, keep the Sabbath in any way at all, or feel the pride, privilege, and glory of belonging to a nation unique in history? Why do so many intermarry with no thought of bringing their spouses or children into the Jewish community?

Largely, I believe, because Judaism itself strikes so many Jews nowadays as strange and forbidding, or obsolete and pointless, or so vague and bland that its basic ethical teachings seem like mere truisms.

Which is hardly surprising, and gets us right back to the purpose of this book. Comprehending Judaism requires that we see it whole. The same holds for any object—*Hamlet,* baseball, the American constitution; "comprehending" *means* "seeing whole." But most books on Judaism—and this is no reflection on the learning or wisdom of my fellow authors—focus on only one part of the grand scheme. They deal with Jewish prayer, history, ritual, literature, art, theology, philosophy. What we lack is the grand scheme itself: the big picture that encompasses all these elements; the underlying idea.

No author can master all this vast intellectual acreage. Certainly I have not, and never could. Nor is it possible that any one theme can meet our requirements. To see Judaism whole, we need a group of themes—and not just any group will do. Our group must have a special property: when you add up its separate themes in your mind, a vision of the whole must emerge like mist over a lake, or a genie from a magic lamp. The group must be an "emergent system," to borrow a useful term from philosophy and science. The whole must be more than the sum of its parts. A mosaic, for example, is an emergent system. No single tile can make you see the bird, tree, or inscription that is visible when you see all the tiles together, simultaneously. (Augustine uses the image of a mosaic in a broadly related way, borrowed from Plotinus: he describes the universe as a mosaic in which God's presence is manifest only if you see all the tiles together.)[1]

I will present in this book an emergent system of four themes. Each theme in the group must itself have a special property. Each must be an *image*, to be seen directly or imagined. Many people think in images most of the time, and nearly everyone does occasionally. Images are the stuff of thought. None of my four theme-images is a principle that has been formulated by scholars. Each is a thought, taken from its natural setting inside the mind and put down on paper as faithfully as possible. My basic themes take the form of images because Judaism is less a system of belief than a way of living, a particular texture of time. Each of my four themes is a mental image that accumulates over time in the mind of a practicing Jew. Virtually all observant Jews will recognize these themes.

In the past such mental images have rarely been described. Often they are not formulated or reduced to words even in the thinker's own mind. But the time has come; today these theme-images must be described in words.

Why? Because unless the essence of Judaism is written down as plainly as can be, the loosening grip most American Jews maintain on the religion of their ancestors will fail completely, and the community will plummet into the anonymous depths of history. ("How art thou fallen from heaven, O Daystar son of morning!" [Isaiah 14:12].)

For now, Zionism holds the Jewish community together, but cannot do so forever. Zionism—love of the land and the state of Israel—is an integral and foundational part of Judaism. It appears in each one of my themes. Taken on its own, it is a rudimentary religion in itself. Its appeal is direct and emotional, and it has the power to hold Jewish minds in rough alignment during a temporary spiritual power outage. But unless the main generator comes back online, unless Judaism as a whole reemerges in all its grandeur and sublimity, the Jewish community will fall apart. If that should happen, the loss would be mankind's.

These basic image-themes must be written down for another reason too. Jews rarely do well at explaining Judaism to Gentiles. Yet Gentiles have often been curious about this ancient faith, the one great Western religion whose central purpose is *not* to prepare believers for salvation in the life to come but to sanctify life on earth. Some Gentiles are drawn not just by curiosity but by personal attachments or spiritual longings. They, too, need the big picture.

So it is time to write down the essence of Judaism as an "emergent system" of nuanced image-themes, each as richly multilayered as a coppery peach or a vivid blue in a Titian painting built of glaze upon glaze upon glaze. By describing these image-themes, I hope to make it possible for readers to superimpose or synthesize them in their own minds—thereby arriving at Judaism seen whole.

When the destruction of the Second Temple in Jerusalem forced an end to the sacrificial offerings of the priests and Levites, the Talmud asked how *avodah*—God's service—could possibly continue. Its reply: sacrificial offerings must now be replaced by offerings "that are in the heart"—meaning (says the Talmud, Ta'anit 2a), by prayer. Although "prayer" in this passage means specifically the Eighteen Blessings (Judaism's most important prayer), *avodah she'ba'lev,* "service in the heart," came to mean prayer in general. Other authorities connect the phrase "service in the heart" with biblical verses calling for spiritual, heartfelt worship. Rabbi Shimon bar Yohai (to whom I return) uses the phrase in a midrash to explain the verse "to serve Him with all your heart." The medieval commentator and grammarian David Kimchi, known as the Radak, cites the phrase in connection with Isaiah's famous charge to the gravely ill King Hezekiah ("Set thine house in order, for thou shalt die"), and Hezekiah's response: "I beseech thee, O Lord, remember now how I have walked before thee in truth and with a perfect heart" (II Kings 20:1, 20:3). Hezekiah is referring, writes the Radak, to his "service in the heart."

Now, Judaism long ago wrote down its two sacred Torahs, the *Torah she'bikhtav*, or "written Torah," meaning the Torah or Bible proper, and the *Torah she'b'al peh*, the "spoken Torah," meaning the Talmud and associated rabbinic writings. It has yet to write down the *Torah she'ba'lev*, or "Torah of the heart"—Judaism seen whole. Theology in general is less central to Judaism than to the other great Western religions. Practice, the rabbis insist, comes first; illumination later. (In the words of a midrash, "Let a man first do good deeds, and then ask God for knowledge of Torah; let a man first act as the righteous and the upright act, and then let him ask God for wisdom; let a man first grasp the way of humility, and then ask God for understanding.") Rabbi Joseph Dov Soloveitchik, preeminent philosopher of modern rabbinic Judaism, taught that (in Rabbi Isadore Twersky's words), "The religious consciousness is not to be subservient to or derivative from any philosophic impetus." Judaism's views of God and man develop privately in the mind of each active Jew—which makes these beliefs vivid to practicing Jews but hard to communicate to anyone else, Jew or Gentile.

Someday a comprehensive *Torah she'ba'lev* will exist, an authoritative rendering of Judaism-as-a-whole that all will acknowledge. My book is a tentative beginning of a process that one day, God willing, will culminate in a work (no doubt by many authors) that will appear routinely in every Jewish library and that might be called, for short, *Torat ha-lev*, the Torah of the mind and heart.

So this book presents four theme-images of Judaism, laid out in individual chapters. Each of the four captures all of Judaism from a certain angle; each is a microcosm of Judaism.

The four themes answer four basic questions.

First: Why does Judaism have such intricate ceremonies and laws? Why can't Jews treat religion as a personal matter between man and God, with no complex rule-book butting in? And a larger version of the same question: Jewish law covers everything from weddings to legal procedure in criminal cases, from the preparation of kosher food to the exact manner in which a Torah scroll must be written. Is there an underlying idea in all this mass of detail?

My first theme, "Separation," suggests answers.

Second: How can a Jew understand and deal with a God as abstract and indescribable as the unique God of Judaism? Doesn't this pure and deep but difficult view doom Judaism to be a cold, abstruse, forbidding religion, in which man and God are kept apart by an impermeable barrier or an infinite gap? The answers (or at least possible answers) are inherent in my second theme, "Veil."

Third: Insofar as its public ceremonies are conducted by males, normative Judaism seems to be a religion for men. Is Judaism prejudiced against women? Assuming we reject the idea that women are in any way inferior, aren't we forced to demand basic changes to traditional Judaism? Or, in more positive terms: How does Judaism understand sexuality, the family, and relationships between man and woman in general? Answers to these questions emerge from my third theme, "Perfect Asymmetry."

Finally, and hardest by far: The deepest problem any religious believer faces is the question of evil in light of God's justice. Shakespeare framed it best in *Macbeth*, in Macduff's cry of rage and grief when he learns that his wife and children have been murdered. "*Did heaven look on and would not take their part?*"

How can we accept the simultaneous existence of a just, all-powerful God and a merciless world? Judaism's answer—it is not a pat answer, and not everyone will find it easy or even possible to accept—is framed in my final theme, "Inward Pilgrimage."

These, in sum, are my themes and their associated questions: (1) Separation: What is the point of halakha, the Jewish religious law? (2) Veil: How can man be in touch with the transcendent, ineffable Lord as Judaism conceives Him? (3) Perfect asymmetry: What is the family's role in normative Judaism, and is woman's role (as it seems to many people) an inferior role? (4) Inward pilgrimage: How can Judaism reconcile an all-powerful, just, and merciful God with cruel reality?

In addressing these themes I do not attempt to summarize current thinking among theologians and philosophers of Judaism. I attempt instead to summarize Judaism itself. Many of my arguments may strike readers as novel, but I believe that my supporting evidence is solid; readers will judge for themselves.

Now I will reintroduce each of my four themes as an *image*. What sort of image is "separation," or "perfect asymmetry"? I will answer by asking that you build each one in your mind step-by-step. ("My way is to conjure you," says Rosalind in *As You Like It*.) For concreteness, you might imagine yourself in an amphitheater, gazing down at a stage on which shapes appear and sometimes blend together.

"Separation" first. Imagine a man in synagogue holding the Torah wide open overhead, one handle in each hand. (This is the ritual called *hagbah*.) You see him there onstage with his back facing you, scroll toward you, his muscles tensed and arms braced. Now imagine the façade of a great nineteenth century synagogue like Central Synagogue in Manhattan, framed by two identical towers.

These two images occupy the exact same space and blend together: the Torah scroll's two uprights blending into the two towers of the synagogue. As Jews enter the synagogue on Shabbat morning, they seem to disappear through the doors right into the Torah scroll that is stretched tight between the two upright wooden dowels on which the scroll's start and finish are wound. (The two-towers motif originated in churches and mosques, not in the Torah scroll; but Judaism gives the motif a new meaning and force.)

Now imagine the Red Sea split apart to allow the Israelites to escape Egypt into the distance, a wall of water to each side—and let all three images blend together, one water-wall coinciding with each tower and each upright of the Torah. Watch the Israelites passing between the water-walls. They are walking straight into the Torah, *or* into (or toward) the synagogue—and these superimposed images give us a hint (only a hint) that forcing apart, or *separation,* with holiness appearing in the space between, is somehow basic to Judaism. The reasons why are deep and important; here I touch only on the images themselves.

Many more translucent layers can be added to this image of separation. Other ingredients can be added too. Kashrut, for example, is all about separation—between kosher and non-kosher food, kosher meat and kosher dairy, kosher-for-Passover and ordinary kosher. Many Jewish laws and rituals center on the creation of holiness by means of deliberate separation. The multilayered image of separation and holiness we have conjured up gives us a hint that kashrut's significance goes far beyond any antique tribal custom; it is connected to something basic in Judaism.

Now empty the stage for a preliminary glimpse of a second theme-image, "Veil."

In synagogue some man (maybe the same one who held the Torah) prepares to put on his *tallit gadol*, the large tallis that is worn at morning prayer. He holds it above his head and (if there is room) stretches it wide as he says the blessing before the sacred act of draping it round his shoulders. Picture the tallis, a large sheet of cloth—often of white cotton simply decorated with black stripes at each end, with ritual fringes (*tsisit*) at the four corners—stretched high and wide, obscuring (from the waist up) the man who holds it behind and above him.

When he says Judaism's most fundamental prayer, often with the tallis draped over his head, a Jew is instructed in the Talmud to imagine himself in God's presence. The tallis separates him from the imagined presence of the Lord. Now picture the Western Wall in Jerusalem. The Wall is the holiest site in Judaism, but makes for a remarkable shrine because it is blank and undecorated, with exactly nothing within or behind or beyond it; yet Jews feel near to God at the Wall, for many reasons. Tallis and Wall blend together. Each is a blank plane (or "veil") that separates a Jew from (or connects him to) holiness.

Add to these images Moses rejoining the Israelites after meeting God. The most extraordinary man in all history stands before you onstage, but his face is covered: he wears a veil. Because he has just encountered (in some way) the Lord Himself, his face gives off light and people are frightened unless he covers it. (But still you sense a strange luminescence through the weave of the veil.)

This veil of Moses separated the Jews at large from a vivid manifestation of holiness. In the sacred desert tabernacle, and later at the Temple in Jerusalem, the Holy of Holies was curtained off by a pair of veils. These several veils blend with the Western Wall and an ordinary tallis.

Now add a sound instead of an image, the sound of the shofar on Rosh ha-Shanah. The sound is "blank": plays no tune, has no lyrics, speaks no words. The blended images of tallis and Wall, Moses' veil and the curtained-off Holy of Holies, accompanied by the shofar's uncanny sound, give us a hint about sacred veils that seemingly separate (but actually connect) the Jew and his ineffable God. As Judaism understands Him, God is inconceivable yet near at hand. The sacred veil is another of Judaism's basic theme-images.

Clear the stage again, but let Moses with his veiled luminous face return. Moses is there before you, but his face is covered. Superimpose the image of a housewife lighting Shabbat candles near dusk on Friday evening. The candles are set on a table and she stands behind, facing you. She lights the candles and then raises her hands to cover her face. Her covered face blends with Moses' covered face, her hands with Moses' veil. Moses is lit up by his recent encounter with God, the woman by Shabbat candles—which (given the logic of these superimposed images) suggests that God's presence and the lit candles are somehow related; it suggests also that the woman stands in somehow for Moses himself.

Erase those images and reset the stage with the biblical figures of Jacob and Rachel side by side, then Elkhanan and Hannah from the book of Samuel, he blending with Jacob and she with Rachel, and then from the Talmud add Rabbi Akiba and his wife, Rachel: three loving marriages. Let all three men blend into one, and the three women too—and what stands between this man and this wife? Nothing: they are as close as two human beings can be. Yet the rabbis tell us there is something between them: the actual (not imagined!) presence of God, the Shekhinah itself. In Judaism, a husband and wife who love each other are reactive agents so powerful, they virtually blow a hole in the cosmos when you bring them together—and set God's presence right before you.

This picture hints at my third theme: Judaism's ideal of "perfect asymmetry" between man and woman.

Finally, empty the stage once more and picture Abraham atop Mount Moriah with his son at his side. Abraham had been sent to offer Isaac as a sacrifice, but has just sacrificed the ram God wanted (and provided) instead. Facing you, Abraham is too deeply moved to be happy. He holds Isaac against him with both hands, and tears presumably streak the grime of three days' walking, and his eyes are downcast. He has just finished an awful three-day struggle of a journey, one of the hardest any man ever made. But as he stands before us he knows something he never knew before, not only about the Lord but about himself, and the force of his trust in God.

Now superimpose an image of Moses moments before his death. He too is atop a mountain—Mount N'vo at the very edge of (but outside) the land of Israel. As he overlooks the landscape he would certainly—being only human, and knowing the nearness of death—have been looking over his own life, too, and its astonishing conclusion on the doorstep of his goal.

And now watch the Second Temple take shape many centuries later, also on a mountaintop—traditionally in the same place where Abraham stood. (Some archeologists believe that the First Temple was cut into the slope just below the summit.) The Temple was organized as a series of courtyards leading inward toward the innermost spot of all: the empty, cubical room called the Holy of Holies. (In the First Temple the Ark of the Covenant stood there, but it was lost and gone when the Second Temple was built.) The Temple leads you inward, as Abraham's journey to Mount Moriah and Moses' to Mount N'vo must have led them into the depths of their own hearts and souls.

We see the same inward trajectory (please hold in mind the superimposed images of Abraham, Moses, and the Temple, each on a mountaintop) in one of the most important transitions in Jewish history, which I mentioned earlier. The rituals of sacrifice at the Temple's altar were called *avodah*, service. With the Temple gone, what replaces this form of service? *Avodah she'ba'lev*, service of the heart; prayer. The mind turned inward is a state we associate with Abraham on Moriah and Moses at the end of his life; the Temple compound led from outer to inner to inner-more to innermost—yet the Temple itself was a mere way station in Judaism's search for the innermost sacred place of all, where the Lord's service continues to this day—the human mind and heart.

This is a glance at the last of my four themes, "inward pilgrimage."

Empty the stage a last time and recall the start of Moses' career, when he encounters the miraculous bush that burns but is not consumed, and learns the mission and meaning of his life. Imagine the burning bush set directly at stage center. In looking at this bush, Moses is seeing a vision not only of the Lord but of his own psyche. This thornbush that burns but is not consumed is part of the "inward pilgrimage" theme, as I will explain. But it is something else, too—a vision of Judaism itself.

The bush burns but is not consumed; Jews are slaughtered yet Israel is not consumed. ("In every generation they
rise against us," says the Passover Haggadah, wearily.) Judaism
is a passion so intense—listen (just once!) to the prayers at the
close of Yom Kippur—that it *must* burn itself out; yet it burns
on. Israel is a meager thornbush of a nation, small in numbers
(so many Jews having been slaughtered in so many massacres
over so many centuries), beset by murderous enemies on every
side—yet its incandescent certainty in the knowledge of God's
wishes lights up the world. "Come ye and let us walk in the
light of the Lord!" (Isaiah 2:5). "It has been told you O man
what is good, and what the Lord wants of you: only to do justice, love mercy, and walk humbly with your God" (Micah 6:8).
Justice and mercy, humility and sanctity: these are attainable
goals, they *can* be achieved. Yet the thornbush itself suffers unending agonies of fire.

Call back all our visions, and let the burning bush be surrounded by Moses, Abraham, and Isaac on their mountain-
tops, then (in the next ring) Jacob and his Rachel, Elkhanan
and Hannah, Akiba and *his* Rachel, then (opposite each other)
by a woman blessing the Shabbat candles and Moses once
again with his luminous face veiled; then in an outer ring by
the Torah lifted high and (on the other side) a mass of Israelites streaming across the Red Sea.

This might be too much to see all at once. The Israelites
push and stumble forward through the sea-bottom muck, the
flames of Shabbat and of the thornbush feint up and down,
crouch and soar—and perhaps the three couples join hands
and dance around the burning thornbush. If you allow this all
to blend in your mind, you might find yourself asking (with
William Butler Yeats), "O body swayed to music, O brighten-
ing glance, How can we know the dancers from the dance?" Ju-

daism is in fact the dance, not the dancers; not these individuals before you but the ideas they draw, spell, suggest, or signify with their bodies and lives—separation and sanctity, the sacred veil, the perfect asymmetry of man and woman, the inward pilgrimage.

The ultimate purpose of Judaism's descendant religions is—as I have mentioned—to point the way to a life that merits (or is rewarded by) salvation or beatitude in the world to come. But Judaism's basic goal is to show each person how to live so as to make his life holy. There is much rabbinic discussion (often vague) of life after death as the ultimate good in store for those who qualify. But as usual, Maimonides gets to the heart of the matter when he writes, in his Mishnah commentary, that there is nothing wrong with doing the Lord's commandments because of the rewards or punishments you anticipate—until your mind has matured, and you are able to do them purely out of love. A Talmudic passage tells us to "do the commandments just for the sake of doing them" (Nedarim 62a). Jews are instructed to live a godly life for its own sake and for the love of God; to "worship the Lord in the beauty of holiness" (Psalms 29:2).

Thus the Hebrew Bible's most important eschatological vision describes life on earth, not in heaven:

> And it shall come to pass in the last days, that the mountain of the Lord's house shall be established in the top of the mountains, and shall be exalted above the hills; and all nations shall flow unto it.
>
> And many people shall go and say, Come ye, and let us go up to the mountain of the Lord, to the house of the God of Jacob; and He will teach us of his ways, and we will walk in His paths: for out of

Zion shall go forth the law, and the word of the
Lord from Jerusalem.

And He shall judge among the nations, and shall
rebuke many people: and they shall beat their
swords into plowshares, and their spears into prun-
inghooks: nation shall not lift up sword against nation, neither shall they learn war any more. (Isaiah
2:2–4; see also Micah 4:1–4)

Thus also the last words of a dying Jew, directed not to God in
supplication but to the nation and the future in proud reaffir-
mation: "Hear, Israel! The Lord is our God; the Lord is one."

One of Judaism's most important blessings is the *Sheheyanu,* a whole worldview in eleven Hebrew words. "Blessed
art thou, Lord our God, King of the universe, who has granted
us life, sustained us and allowed us to reach this occasion." It is
recited when the shofar is blown on Rosh ha-Shanah, at the
start of the festival of Sukkot, when lighting the first Hanukah
candles and at other holidays; and when you move into a new
house, taste some fruit for the first time in its season, and at
other festive events. Thus life is measured out by a series of sacred and beautiful occasions large and small, and each time we
reach one we say, *Thank God I am alive to experience this moment.* Not ultimate salvation but life itself is God's greatest gift,
and Judaism is a method of grasping this truth not just intellectually but "with all your heart, with all your soul and with
all your might" (Deuteronomy 6:5).

The occasions when *Sheheyanu* seems called for but is
not recited speak eloquently, too, of Judaism's central preoccupation. The last two days of Passover are festivals in themselves, commemorating the crossing of the Red Sea and the destruction of Egypt's army. But we do not recite *Sheheyanu,*

because we are not to rejoice over the death of any of God's creatures. ("Rejoice not when thine enemy falleth, and let not thine heart be glad when he stumbleth" [Proverbs 24:17]. The angels were moved to break out in song when Egypt's army perished, but—says the Talmud—God stopped them: "How can you sing while my creatures are drowning in the sea?" [Megillah 10b].)

Judaism's preoccupation with life is part of the burning bush—a plain plant rooted in plain soil that lives on as the seat of God's revelation and never succumbs to fire, or disappears into a higher realm.

The fiery word of God still thins and thickens, crouches and leaps high and hiss-and-crackles in the Jewish nation's thornbush bones. The prodded logs erupt; they fill the air with fire seeds sifting downward to become torn petals that perfume the earth with vague awareness of the scent of God. And all our martyrs, dead in the dust, still shout the Lord is One, His Name One—you *can* hear them, if you try.

Return one last time to my four basic themes, each in the form of an image (in some cases an unfamiliar kind of image). Images are, as I have noted, an important medium of thought. But many scholars believe that Judaism is allergic to images.

This alleged hostility is well known; it is connected to the strong biblical prohibition against graven images of the Lord. Judaism "fears the image," writes the critic and literary philosopher George Steiner, saying what many people believe. Judaism "distrusts the metaphor."

Exactly wrong. It is true that during some (only some) periods of Jewish history, rabbis forbade the depiction of the human body. The prohibition in the Ten Commandments has been interpreted in different ways at different times, depending on whether or not paganism and idolatry seemed like actual threats to the Jewish community. In any case, "image" is a large idea, and associating it only with depictions of the human body seems impossibly naïve. Judaism is in fact passionately attached to images; they are its favorite means of expression.

Even a quick glance at the Bible makes it plain that Jewish thought luxuriates in vivid imagery: the dove with a torn olive branch in its beak, the burning bush, the split-open sea, the mountain on fire like a torch, the valley of dry bones, Aaron's rod, the writing on the wall, the chariot of fire. Consider the finely wrought visual detail in the Bible's description of the desert tabernacle; even the manifest of raw materials is visually dazzling: "Gold and silver and bronze; and ultramarine, and purple, and scarlet yarn and fine linen, and goat's hair; and rams' hides dyed earth-red, tanned leather, and acacia wood. Oil for lamplight; spices for anointing oil and for fragrant smoking incense. Onyx, stones for setting—for the ephod and the breastplate" (Exodus 25:3–7). The details that follow are complete enough to have made it possible to build elaborate modern models.

Much of medieval art in Europe is a celebration of biblical imagery carried out with rare single-mindedness—both chivalry and royalty required warriors and kings as precedents who were heroic *and* godly; such heroes were to be found in the Hebrew Bible only.

The medieval Christian artist translates biblical images directly from words into paint, sculpture, tapestry, glass. Innumerable medieval artworks show Moses with the tablets, Aaron with his rod, David with his lyre, Noah and the ark and the flood, Daniel in the lion's den, and many others. Above all, the tree of Jesse: "And there shall come forth a rod out of Jesse,

and a branch shall grow out of his roots, and the spirit of the
Lord shall rest upon him" (Isaiah 11:1).

Naturally these images are interpreted very differently by
Jews and Christians. Nonetheless, had Jews "feared the image,"
had classical Jewish literature not supplied rich word imagery
for Gentile artists to translate into other media, medieval
Christian art as we know it would have been impossible.[2] The
Hebrew Bible underlies other aspects of medieval art too. Biblical descriptions of the desert Tabernacle, the Celestial Temple
of Ezekiel, and especially Solomon's Temple were regarded as
divine instructions to medieval church builders. "The dimen-
sions of the Solomonic Temple seem to have been viewed as
ideal, because divinely inspired, proportions for the Christian
sanctuary."[3]

In recent centuries, the West has come to appreciate the
beauty and profundity of biblical poetry. Poetry, too, requires
imagery. In his book *Prophet and Poet* (1965), on the Bible and
the growth of English romanticism, Murray Roston writes
that William Blake (1757–1827) "drew his store of images
straight from the Scriptures. . . . The innocent lambs of the
Psalmist, the fruitful vine under which the ancient Hebrew
rested, the deceitful serpent of Genesis . . . even the harlots
symbolic of Israel's shame and infidelity are woven into the
tapestry of [Blake's] *Songs of Innocence and Experience* without a trace of embarrassment or apology." Over the long centuries since pagan Europe turned gradually Christian, even
European artists and thinkers who were ignorant of Judaism
or hostile to it (as virtually all medieval Christian artists were)
have been deeply influenced by classical Jewish imagery. (The
composer Richard Wagner, for example, was an anti-Semite;
but the spectacular conclusion of *Tannhäuser* is built on the
image of Aaron's rod bursting into bloom, and the opera

closes with a repeated *Alleluia!*, a Latin transliteration of the
Hebrew word.)

Christianity has one main emblem or graphic symbol
and two or three secondary ones. Judaism has four main em-
blems and six others that are nearly as important. Some are
old, some fairly new; their origins are varied; but all are in use
today. Such image counting doesn't prove anything in itself,
but gives us something to think about.

Judaism's basic images are the seven-branched Temple
menorah; the six-pointed "star of David"; the tables of the Ten
Commandments; the four Hebrew letters of God's proper
name (these letters appear often in synagogue interiors, not as
a word to be read but as a symbol to be grasped as a unit). The
other six, also ubiquitous in Jewish art and architecture, are the
crown of Torah; the lion of Judah; the shofar, usually a ram's
horn; the lulav and etrog of the festival of Sukkot; the open
Torah scroll in outline; and a pair of hands upheld side by side
in the distinctive gesture of the priestly blessing. Many others
are fairly common, or used to be. France is said to have gotten
its fleur-de-lys from the Crusaders, who took it from the styl-
ized lily that was a popular motif in ancient Israelite Jerusalem.

Judaism "fears the image"? Maybe George Steiner fears it.
Possibly it is just because the Jewish mind is so exuberantly
visual that graven images of the Lord are so forcefully pro-
hibited.

Words are coarse tools for expressing images, but they
are usually the only tools we have. Yet words are only a starting
point. Unconsciously and instinctively, the reader fills in the
blanks and adds detail. Consider "the first fine day of spring":
the reader imagines far more than the author has written. Language launches thought as a boy on shore launches a rowboat.
An image in the mind floats a long way out before coasting to

a stop. Language is restricted symbolically to solid ground, but we spend much of our mental lives on the water wrapped up in imagery, beyond the reach of language.

It is strange, even paradoxical, that although ours is said to be a "visual age," modern thinkers have mostly failed to grapple with mental images and their significance. We have yet to understand the "language" of images: how simple ones are combined; how images tell stories. Look up "mental images" in the respected *Cambridge Dictionary of Philosophy* (1995) and you will learn that "because the ontological status of such images and the nature of their properties are obscure, many philosophers have rejected mental images."

Which is tough luck for those philosophers, because mental images are, as I have said, the very stuff of thought for large numbers of human beings. And Judaism in particular has always preferred the concrete to the abstract, the simple, vivid picture ("Look now toward heaven, and tell the stars, if thou be able to number them: So shall thy seed be") to the abstract theoretical proposition.

The four theme-images I am about to discuss are hardly all-inclusive. On the contrary—the same methods can be used to discover other themes, too. But I do believe that these particular four rank among Judaism's most important. It happens also that my four themes correspond roughly to the four sections of the *Arba'ah Turim* and the *Shulhan Arukh*, Judaism's basic legal texts. One deals with everyday life, one with our knowledge of God, one with the family and relations between man and woman, and one with justice on earth.

Each of my theme-images could be the subject of a kindergarten class or a graduate seminar. Different Jews interpret them differently, but all Jews share them.

I could go further. These haunting images don't merely belong to Jews; they are the *Iliad,* or Chartres, or the *Goldberg Variations.* They belong to mankind. Every human being deserves the chance to see and understand them.

So we turn now to Judaism and its Torah of the mind and heart—its fragrant secret garden where one might walk "in the cool of the day," its beautiful and mysterious hidden courtyard that has always been closed by its very nature to all but observant Jews. "Awake O north wind and approach O south; breathe upon my garden, that its spices may flow forth" (Song of Songs 4:16).

# II

# Separation

**W**hy does Judaism have such intricate ceremonies and laws? Why can't religion be a personal matter between man and God, with no complex rule book butting in?

Traditionally such questions were raised by Christians in the process of arguing for Christianity's superiority. Nowadays they are asked more often by Jews who have rejected normative Judaism for some liberal or reformed variety, or who have left Judaism altogether. But whoever asks, and whatever his motive, the questions are central and need answering.

The answers are built into Judaism's very fabric. I will start with a physical gesture in synagogue. From there the trail leads straight into the separation theme, and our questions are answered as we emerge on the far side.

I have already mentioned the gesture called *hagbah*, lifting high: after each reading of the Torah in synagogue, the open scroll is lifted overhead so that the whole congregation can see it. Three columns of text must be visible. Those in the congregation see the wide-open scroll supported by two strong, tensed arms. (They had better be strong. The scroll is heavy.)

Why is this moment so evocative and resonant? Where have we met something like it before? When the children of Israel fled Egypt through the rolled-open sea toward Sinai and the gift of the Torah, the waters were "piled-up, erected upright." The sea became "a wall to their right and their left" (Exodus 14:22).

The act of *hagbah* recalls these "twin verticals" and others as well. Think also, as I have mentioned, of the matching towers that frame the fronts of many large nineteenth century synagogues: the Central Synagogue in midtown Manhattan, for instance, was built in 1872 and inspired by the gigantic Dohany Street synagogue in Budapest. Synagogue architects did not consciously mimic the shafts of the raised scroll; they borrowed the matching-spires motif from churches and mosques. But these spires, when they are done properly, have a resonant richness they never had in any mosque or church. They turn the plain act of entering a synagogue into a living metaphor: each new arrival disappears into the space between the two raised standards, right into the Torah itself.

This already tells us something significant: in Judaism, holiness and beauty are intertwined. Other religions have encased their sacred ceremonial in far more elaborate shells, but Judaism requires that the ceremonies themselves (and the words that go along with them, and the thoughts that go with the words) be intrinsically beautiful. Why? Because Judaism is above all a religion of joy. "Shout unto the Lord, all the earth! Worship Him in joy, come before Him in song!" (Psalms 100:1–2). Beauty is a powerful creator of joy ("Worship the Lord in the beauty of holiness" [Psalms 29:2]). The rabbis instruct us to carry out each commandment as beautifully as we can; *hiddur mitzvah*, the beautification of a commandment (or *mitzvah*), is a rabbinic imperative. We cannot speak of Judaism without speaking about beauty.

This, then, is beautiful: walking into a double-spired syn-agogue as if you were entering the sacred Torah itself, merging with the sacred text. Or performing *hagbah* and thereby echo-ing two acts of Moses simultaneously, holding open the Torah as he held open the sea; presenting the scroll as he did the tablets.

*Why* beautiful? Because communal memories just be-neath the surface make these acts resonate—like the unex-pectedly rich, strong, musical sound of a violin when you play one note and the whole instrument acts as a soundboard for the single vibrating string.[1] Furthermore, these acts open vis-tas right to the heart of Judaism—and vistas are thrilling. As long ago as 1947, the English art historian John Harvey wrote (in *Gothic England*) that "modern critics tell us to avoid the terms of beauty and ugliness, but surely this is to dehumanize humanity. Man ever has, and ever must, respond to beauty whether he analyze it or no."

Back to "Separation." In the beginning, says the book of Gen-esis, was chaos—*tohu va'vohu*. Chaos means mixed-together-ness, *un*-separation. To banish chaos, you must separate. God *separates* (during the story of Creation) light from dark, the waters above from the waters beneath, day from night. To make room for the sky and earth and man, He forces apart the chaotic primeval waters. The waters are swept (pushed, shoved, driven—a gigantic gesture) up high and down low. "God said, let there be a firmament in the midst of the waters; and let it separate between water and water. And God made the firmament, and separated the water beneath the firmament and the water above the firmament; and it was so. And God called the firmament 'heavens'" (Genesis 1:6–7).

Creation and Exodus are a pair. When Israel is born at the Red Sea, God separates the waters once again, just long enough for Israel to escape into nationhood. God forces an opening: "Raise your rod and stretch out your hand over the sea," He tells Moses, "and split it" (Exodus 14:16). The forced-open seas stand upright in two walls and then tumble closed over the pursuing Egyptians, no doubt with a roar and a crash and a cool mist rising afterward, with the taste and smell of brackish water.

Creation is the story of God's *ruach*—"breath," "spirit"— suspended over "the face of the water," or "the deep," or the "seas," and of "dry land" appearing in the midst of this water. Exodus is a story of this same *ruach* pushing back the sea and of "dry land" appearing "in the midst of the sea." Both times God's basic act is the same—forcing waters apart so that the world, or Israel, can come to life. Creation and Exodus are two versions of one story.

(Harmony requires that we hear related notes together. The harmonic beauty of Judaism is based on related events like Creation and Exodus speaking simultaneously.)

Birth itself is separation, parturition. "Let there be a firmament in the midst of the water; let it separate water from water" (Genesis 1:6). The waters pull apart leaving virgin emptiness, wet like any newborn. The birth imagery is explicit: the spreading apart, the broken waters. (Now we have a three-part chord: the world born from the black waters of chaos, Israel from the sea, a child from the oceanic human body.) Later the Land of Israel will be made ready the same way earth itself is created, by the Lord's forcing an opening. Powerful agents will be swept apart—agents that can and will rush (headlong, hurtling) back together if they get the chance.

Two acts of cosmic separation underlie Creation and Exodus. Both times the space God creates is like a hole in the water—a forced, temporary opening in the teeth of nature. Left to its own devices, nature flows together. Nature is muck, mixing, impurity, unseparation, chaos.

Noah, "a man righteous in his generation," lived in a morally mixed-up world. In one culminating example of earthly corruption, "The sons of God saw that the daughters of men were beautiful, and took themselves wives" (Genesis 6:2)—a mysterious, ominous story of mixing, unseparation, impurity. Somehow, creatures who should have been separate came together.

When the Lord decides to destroy the corrupt world of Noah's day, He need only let the upper and lower waters rush (and roar and tumble) back together from above the earth and beneath: from "the floodgates of the heavens" and "the springs of the deep." Noah's flood and the rushing-together Red Sea waters are (again) two instances of one event. Israel's escape as Egypt's army drowns under reuniting waters recalls Noah's escape as a corrupt civilization drowns under reuniting waters. A dark, foreboding chord.

God uses separation as an act of sanctification and unseparation (*un*creation) as a tool of punishment. Water isn't necessary. When the men of Shinar try to build a tower to heaven (the tower of Babel), God scatters them across the earth like skittering bowling pins and turns human language itself into chaos, into a mixed-up mess.

Birth is separation; death, unseparation. Flesh rejoins (is mixed into) the earth. In biblical times, the dry bones of the

dead were themselves intermixed—heaped up in what archeologists call charnel piles. The Torah of the Heart turns these
mundane facts into universal truth, into a powerful theme-
image of creation-separation-life eternally at the edge of a
monstrous pounding waterfall—with man (at God's urging)
stubbornly refusing to slip over the edge, pulling defiantly
against the current. This hard yet joyful pulling is what Judaism means when it tells us to choose life—and gives us an
important clue regarding the centrality of rabbinic law in Judaism, as we will see.

Beauty requires pattern. Repeated acts of separation form
a pattern in *Torat ha-lev*. Chaos is the opposite of sanctity *and*
beauty. Shakespeare says so in "Venus and Adonis": "He being
dead, with him is beauty slain, / And, beauty dead, black chaos
comes again." The same thought is repeated less explicitly but
more majestically in *Othello:* "Perdition catch my soul, but I do
love thee! And when I love thee not, chaos is come again."

"Be separate!" This might have been Moses' command to the
waters of the Red Sea. Issuing commands to nature was (after
all) part of his job; during Israel's desert wanderings, he is told
to command a rock to yield water. But in fact he did not speak
to the sea. "Be separate!" is the rabbis' version of a commandment in the Torah: "Make yourselves holy and be holy, because
I am holy" (Leviticus 11:44). A midrash remarks, "'Ye shall be
holy'—as I am holy, be you holy; as I am separate, so be you
separate" (Sifra 57b).

"Be holy." The standard English lexicon of biblical Hebrew (Brown, Driver, and Briggs, or BDB, 1907), gives the following derivation for the Hebrew *kadosh*, holy: "possibly the
original idea is separation, withdrawal." Why? Holiness is a
spiritual idea, separation a mere physical gesture. Holiness is

ordinarily defined in abstract, theological terms. The word *holiness* "indicates the highest value or—more precisely—what can be said by men (or angels) when God comes immediately to mind, as in Isaiah 6:3: 'Holy, holy, holy is the Lord of hosts.'"[2] Why should "be holy" mean (as the rabbis suggest) "be separate"?[3]

Holy things are of course set apart from daily life—from rough handling, dirt, and indignity. But it is also true that if you start with chaos, you must separate to create. Creation means separation, and the Creator is holy. So it is only natural that holiness and the act of separation (of defying chaos) are connected.

Because God is the Creator and man's central obligation is to imitate God, it becomes *man's* duty to create. Rabbi Joseph Dov Soloveitchik writes that "when a Jew on the Sabbath eve recites the *kiddush,* the sanctification over the wine, he testifies not only to the existence of a Creator but also to man's obligation to become a partner with the Almighty in the continuation and perfection of His creation." To be a scientist, artist, or intellectual creator can thus be an expression, in Judaism, of the highest sort of piety.[4] Returning to the obligation to create: few people can achieve this kind of intellectual creativity. Most Jews fulfill their duty to create symbolically, by performing acts of separation. Robert Frost wrote that "something there is that doesn't love a wall." That "something" is nature, and Jews build and rebuild walls because they are commanded to struggle against nature; to choose life.

Here we move a step closer to answering the questions with which this chapter began. Jewish religious law is complex. Halakha makes hundreds of seemingly unrelated demands—some moral and others sacramental, some rational and others incomprehensible, some applicable only in the Land of Israel and others that apply everywhere. But when we look from the right angle, all these laws cohere and we see *separation* as the unifying idea—and a basic theme of Judaism's Torah of the heart. And once we see the chain of meaning that ties life to holiness, holiness to separation, and separation to halakha, we can understand halakha's fundamental importance to Judaism.

In the prescriptive legislation of the Torah, yoking together or crossbreeding different animal species is forbidden. Sowing different types of seed together is forbidden, and so are certain types of grafting. Mixing wool and linen in clothing is forbidden. These laws are collectively called *kil'ayim* and are classified by the rabbis among the Lord's inexplicable decrees (*hukkim*). Observant Jews take them for granted, but others find them (along with kashrut itself) mysterious, opaque, and primitive; which is understandable.

It would be absurd for me to claim that I can explain what the rabbis cannot. I certainly can't explain why these *particular* mixtures are forbidden. But I can explain why any such mixture might be forbidden: because separation is halakha's unifying idea. Because any mixture (of different animals, seeds, fibers) compromises the symbolic walls of separation God has built everywhere against chaos—His dikes against an ever-impending flood.

Never again, God has promised, will the earth be flooded by water. But it might be flooded, again and again, by evil. Halakha allows us to reclaim a space of sanctity from moral chaos.

Jews are not to mix with the pagan peoples of Canaan: "Separate yourselves from the peoples of the land!" (Ezra 10:11, and similar verses). Men are not to dress like women, or women like men (Deuteronomy 22:5).[5] Many were surprised at the vehemence with which Rabbi Soloveitchik, who epitomized everything logical and humane in Orthodox Judaism, affirmed the requirement that men and women must sit separately in synagogue. But one does not lightly pull up and toss out a rule whose roots reach as deep into Judaism as this one's. Nor do we pry out and destroy mosaic tiles without understanding their part in the whole image.

(An individual might be incapable, physically or spiritually, of keeping all the commandments; the rabbis understood this perfectly. But it is a different thing to impose one's own limitations on Judaism by declaring the laws one cannot keep to be invalid or superseded, to be *non*-laws. Your being a Jew depends in the last analysis on your beliefs, not on the extent to which you follow the commandments: "When someone believes in all the fundamental Jewish doctrines," writes Maimonides in his Mishnah commentary, "he is part of the Jewish community." And you are part of the normative, Orthodox community if your *beliefs* make you a part, even if your practices fall short. "As long as a Jew maintains his tie with the Jewish people and the Torah, though he be not fully observant, he is our brother and compatriot," writes Howard I. Levine from the Orthodox viewpoint.[6] The nineteenth century scholar Rabbi Naftali Tsvi Yehuda Berlin, called the N'tziv, rejected the idea that the Orthodox community should hold itself apart from non-observant Jews: "This advice is as fatal as a sword wound in the body of our nation.")

More fundamental still to the separation theme are the rabbinic elaborations of kosherness or kashrut (for example, milk and most kinds of meat must be separated) and of family purity (husband and wife must be sexually separated, periodically). Even more fundamental is the Sabbath, a separation in time (as I discuss below) that is tied explicitly in the Torah to Creation *and* Exodus, the two "primal separations."

For thousands of years halakha has been opaque to all but the handful of practicing Jews in this world, who have obeyed God's commandments and kept the *Torat ha-lev* in their minds and hearts. But what does halakha *mean?* What does it do? The answer is that it transforms Jewish life into a richly symbolic artwork whose theme, *separation,* recurs in countless variations and whose ultimate subject is sanctity and the struggle of joyous life against cruelty, decay, and death.

So separation is more than a theme; it is a microcosm of Judaism as a whole. Now we can add more translucent layers to this deepening image.

As the Jew is separate from the non-Jew, man is separate from all other creatures. (The prayer book addresses God: "You separated man from the beginning.") And the good man is separate from the rest: "the Lord hath set apart the pious man as His own" (Psalms 4:4). "Do not follow a multitude to do evil," says the Torah (Exodus 23:2).

Nothing is easier than to blend with the mass. Nothing is more natural than to pull down the walls, be one of the guys, join the gang. Nothing is harder or less natural than to hold yourself separate. But the Talmud says: "In a place where there are no men, strive to be a man." Separate yourself from the multitude. To separate the waters of chaos, or yourself from the mob, are unnatural acts of holiness.

The struggle between chaos and separation (chaos and sanctity, chaos and beauty, chaos and life) is constant and ongoing. Left to itself, the world goes back to chaos. Nature pulls down all walls and erases all separations. Maintaining sacred separation is an ongoing fight, requiring a constant outpouring of energy—like holding the rolled-open Torah high, or keeping your rowboat from slipping over a waterfall. There is no sanctity without struggle and sweat.

Many non-observant Jews assume that "it must be hard to observe all those religious regulations." In a sense they are right. To stand fast against the gravitational pull of nature and the crowd and cruelty and death *must* be hard. Moreover, they say, nature seems benign and is overwhelmingly beautiful. Why stand against it?

In fact Judaism does not ask that man ignore nature's beauty. Just the opposite: the rabbis require that blessings be said when we encounter natural wonders—a beautiful tree, a rainbow, the ocean. Man is forbidden to abuse nature. Here is a midrash: "At the time the Holy One, blessed be He, created the first man, He took him and showed him again all the plants of the Garden of Eden and said to him—look at My work, how beautiful and blessed! And everything I created, I created for your sake. Beware that you do not damage or destroy My universe. For if you damage it, there is no one to repair it afterward."

And nature's beauty is God's beauty. "The heavens tell God's glory, the work of His hands is told by the firmament. . . . In them He has put a tent for the sun, who is like a bridegroom departing the wedding canopy—rejoicing like a hero to run his course" (Psalms 19:1–2, 6).

Is it possible to be thrilled by nature yet not be (even in the slightest) a pagan worshipper of nature? Yes; but it takes concentration and discipline. To borrow a daring image from the Psalm I have just quoted, a Jew's relationship to nature is like a man's to a beautiful woman he desires but never takes to bed. The Jew's relationship to nature has passion, has tension, and is never consummated. A Jew has reverence for nature as God's work but he works against nature when he creates (or re-creates) separation—and must hold himself separate from nature, not do what is easy and blend in.

For man and nature to blend together is the end of sanctity and life. "What if we were someday to break down the difference between a man and his environment?," asked the philosopher Paul Ziff (1960). "Then someday we would wake up and find that we are robots." "In death I am pluralized, converted from one to many. I become my remains. I merge with my environment."[7]

Maimonides writes in the *Mishneh Torah* (1.4.2): "What is the way to love and revere Him? At the time a man understands His great and wonderful deeds and creations, and sees in them a wisdom without compare and without end, *instantly* he loves and praises and glorifies and yearns deeply to know the Great Name, as David says: 'my being thirsts for God, for the living Lord' (Psalms 42:3)."

I have emphasized "instantly"; it is the key word. Contemplating God's creation doesn't make you *conclude* that God is great, it lifts and staggers you—a man "recoils startled," writes Maimonides. Coleridge has a different but related thought. "Read the first chapter of Genesis without prejudice, and you will be convinced at once." If you are "convinced," you make a decision. If you are "convinced *at once*," the decision makes you.

Yet halakha demands that we travel upstream against the current, against and away from nature. Jews admire the beauties of nature over their shoulders, so to speak, as they pull hard in the other direction.

Of course, the sentimental modern view of nature as lyrically gentle and benign shows merely that modern man knows nothing about it. (Most "modern men" visit nature occasionally, but never stay long.) "Death by violence, death by cold, death by starvation—these are the normal endings of the stately and beautiful creatures of the wilderness." Thus wrote Theodore Roosevelt, America's great naturalist-President, roughly a century ago. The force of death appears in many forms. Some of the subtlest, deepest aspects of Judaism follow from the command to resist that force.

To choose life and resist death is in one sense deliberate futility. No matter what you choose, death is what you get. But Jews are commanded to choose life anyway. Each time a Jew makes a sacred separation, gazes through one, or marches into one, he proclaims his defiance of chaos and nature and death—and acts against them (on however small a scale), replacing one stone of the wall that nature continuously tears down.

In short, Judaism rejects both the anti-nature bias of ancient gnosticism (which flourished in the first couple of centuries of the common era) and the pro-nature (verging on pagan) bias of modern civilization. It's impossible not to be moved and sometimes overwhelmed by nature. But Judaism's Torah of the Heart insists that nature and man must be separate.

To separate yourself from nature is to imitate God, the "Separator"—as He is called in the blessings that mark the end of the Sabbath or a holiday and the resumption of ordinary time. God separates, say these blessings, "between holy and profane, between light and dark, between Israel and other nations, between the seventh day and the six days of creation. Blessed art Thou O Lord, Who separates between holy and profane."

To be a "separator" can mean separating yourself from the world around you, making a social separation. It can mean opening a gap in the cosmos. It can even mean creating a gap in time. There is no other way to understand the Sabbath, which starts with a blessing linking Shabbat to Creation and Exodus; ends with a ceremony in which we bless God-the-Sacred-Separator.

We plunge now into a different type of separation—a separation in time. These new translucent images will further deepen our microcosm, giving us a better picture of Judaism as a whole and simultaneously helping to answer our initial question about the centrality of religious law in Judaism.

Shabbat (or "Shabbes," or "the Sabbath") is the ultimate expression of the theme-image of separation. Shabbat is designed not merely to separate man from the burdens of daily life but to take him outside time. But no one can step through that exit door unthinkingly. A Beethoven sonata can transport you to the rim of the universe—if you listen actively and enter into the music. *Torat ha-lev* can take you outside time—if you play an active part.

For Judaism, earning your living is a necessary burden. It is a dignified burden—"Torah study alongside worldly pursuits is beautiful," says the Talmud—but it is a burden all the same. "In the sweat of thy face shalt thou eat bread, till thou return unto the ground; for out of it wast thou taken: for dust thou art, and unto dust shalt thou return" (Genesis 3:19).

In the *Torat ha-lev*, the idea that anyone would find "fulfillment" in a worldly career is ridiculous. One way Judaism demonstrates this absurdity is by providing an exit door that lets you step outside daily life as naturally as you might step from an overheated house onto a cool porch. Once you are outside you can watch ordinary life screech past like a runaway train. In this area and others, Judaism's comment on contemporary attitudes is simple: they are wrong. No, do *not* teach your children to aspire to brilliant careers. Teach them to learn

Torah, get married and rear faithful Jewish children, and do good deeds.[8] Next to these aspirations, careers are trivial.

Shabbat begins on Friday evening with candlelight and blessings over a raised wine cup and braided bread loaves. Shabbat ends on Saturday night with blessings, again, over a raised wine cup by the light of a braided, many-wicked candle. Symbolically we might almost be frozen in time from start to finish, blessing God at each end in candlelight with cup raised, as if no time had passed. Shabbat is, after all, a gap or hole in time. But notice also how the end resonates with the beginning, and the harmony that results when you hear them together.

Here is a beauty of rhythms, patterns, harmonies, resonant symbols, apt to be felt subliminally more than explicitly. The beauty of *Torat ha-lev* is built into the framework, not added like decorative touches to a finished house. But one way or other, Jews do feel the beauty of their Torah of the Heart; thus the note of exultation that is so typical of Jewish prayer. Shabbat observance at the synagogue begins on Friday evening with Psalm 95, sung by the leader to a soaring simple melody: "Come let us sing to the Lord, let us shout aloud to the Rock of our Salvation!"

The Sabbath is a sacred gap in time. But it must be braced with strong laws or it will be overwhelmed by daily life and close like a hole in the water. It is hard to open a sacred gap (however temporary) in time *or* nature; in some sense it is hard even for God. "When God divided the Red Sea for Israel," says a midrash, "it was heard of from one end of the universe to the other." Keeping the Sabbath is (in its way) just as hard, just as amazing a defiance of the natural order as forcing the Red Sea open. It is hard to separate yourself from the world at large. Hard to pull free from your daily life. Hard to carry out all the holiness-creating steps that Shabbat requires. (In this era of cell phones and e-mail, it is harder than ever.)

It is *supposed* to be hard. It takes effort and transforms you. In synagogue a man lifts the Torah scroll by its handles, raising it high and rolled apart—opening a vista to the heart of Judaism—a sacred gap with radiant sanctity streaming through, like sunlight through a chasm leading all the way back to the start of time. But how long can he hold it there? A Torah scroll is heavy. Not long. To hold open time itself is even harder.

Each theme-image—each element or chapter of *Torat ha-lev*—has many facets (like a cut gem) or—to continue with the established metaphor—many translucent images to be superimposed in your own mind. Shabbat is one image of separation and the Red Sea is another. To superimpose these two images alone suggests that Jews escape into Shabbat as urgently as they once fled into the split-open sea; and emerge as transformed as the Israelites did then.

To fulfill God's commandments is difficult. But observant Jews rarely feel burdened by the effort. To see why, consider one of the liturgy's most haunting phrases. Jews ask of God that He "spread over us *sukkat shlomekha,* the shelter of Your peace." God's commandments seem to intrude into every corner of life, but those who observe them feel the shelter of His peace overspreading them like shade on a hot day. The German-Jewish thinker Franz Rosenzweig "needed no theological theory" to sustain his faith in God; he believed that "life itself—lived under the law—testified to the presence of the divine."[9]

Even non-observant Jews are sometimes aware that keeping the commandments, whether you have faith or not, creates a "shelter of peace." In the words of Ludwig Wittgenstein (the eminent twentieth-century philosopher of Jewish descent): "Life can educate one to a belief in God. And *experiences* too are what bring this about.... Experiences, thoughts—life can force this concept on us."

Separation is the opposite of mixing. Yet once the sacred gap is (briefly) opened, a sort of mixing results. Man goes to meet God, God to meet man. The Sabbath, say the rabbis, is a foretaste of *olam ha'ba,* the world to come. Jews rush out like surging water through the forced-open gap in time, to live for a moment in a paradise outside the walls of the universe. The historian Yosef Yerushalmi writes that the Sabbath "came to be experienced as a day beyond the bounds of historical time, and eventually even as a weekly anticipation of the end of time." If all Israel were to keep *one* Sabbath perfectly, say the rabbis of the Talmud, the messiah would come. God's messenger would enter through the forced-open gap. (Rabbi Shimon bar Yohai differs: if all Israel were to keep *two* Sabbaths perfectly.)

The ceremony that concludes the Sabbath is called (as I have mentioned) "separation," *havdalah.* God uses the Sabbath to open a gap in the week as you might snip a gold ring and force the cut ends apart. But observant Jews do not simply keep the Sabbath and then, when it is over, let it lapse. Shabbat is not over until we say the havdalah blessing, thereby returning back over the threshold between sacred and profane—or stepping back into time.

Shabbat is not the only occasion when Jews step out of and then back into time. The Jewish calendar holds other such events.

The ten days starting on Rosh ha-Shanah (the New Year) and ending on Yom Kippur (the Day of Atonement) form another sacred gap in time. The rabbis understood these two holidays and the "days of awe" between them in terms of a held-open gate. Through this open gate man reaches toward God and God toward man. "Even though penitence and appeal are always beautiful," writes Maimonides, "in the ten days between Rosh ha-Shanah and Yom Kippur they are more beautiful, and are accepted immediately." While the gate is open, the possibility of divine forgiveness beats like bright sunlight on the Jewish nation, and Israel is urged to come in; in Hebrew, "penitence" and "return" are the same word. "Open to me the gates of righteousness. I will enter them, praising the Lord" (Psalms 118:19).

The Talmud describes three judgment books that are opened on Rosh ha-Shanah. The books of the wholly righteous and wholly wicked needn't stay open long; in such cases judgment is easy. But the third book, for the rest of us, stays open until the Day of Atonement: "Man is judged on Rosh ha-Shanah and his decree is sealed on Yom Kippur." As the Bible itself makes perfectly clear, Jews do *not* believe that good men's lives will be happy and bad men's unhappy. A character named Job rejected that view, and his rejection stands for all time. But the image of judgment books opening and shutting captures a state of mind. To live a life of intense self-examination is beyond most of us, but to live that way for ten days each year, from Rosh ha-Shanah to Yom Kippur, might be (just barely) possible.

The ceremony that ends the Sabbath dwells on God the Separator, Who opens sacred gaps; likewise the ceremony called *ne'ilah*—"closing"—at the end of Yom Kippur. Originally this "closing" meant the actual gates of the Temple compound in Jerusalem. (The Temple survives in countless ways, suspended for all time within the language and liturgy of Judaism.) By developing the metaphors of divine judgment books and heavenly gates, the rabbis connect this physical closing with the metaphoric closing of a sacred gap in time. At the end of Yom Kippur, the prayer book speaks urgently of the cosmic gap and how temporary it is, how necessarily, *intrinsically* impermanent. (In old texts without modern refinements like italics for emphasis, we must listen to the implied tone so that nuances don't escape us.) "Open to us the gate at the time of the gate-closing, for the day fades, the day is fading—the sun sets, fading—let us enter Your gates!"

Over the years this connection has grown more explicit. A gap is closing, a door shutting, a separation disappearing— we must get through! A large part of the ne'ilah service is typically performed before the open ark. Ordinarily the ark is kept open (revealing the sacred Torah scrolls inside) for brief periods only. But it stays open for a long time during ne'ilah.

This unaccustomed, drawn-out opening focuses our attention on the still-open but soon-to-shut gates of judgment. During ne'ilah we say imploringly (we the exhausted, fasting congregation, fired-up spiritually, throwing off sparks)—this is the climax of the long Yom Kippur prayers, of the whole ten "days of awe"—"You give your hand to sinners; Your right hand is outstretched to receive penitents"—to gather or pull (or drag) them through the closing gates. Once again, here is the beauty of sympathetic vibration; of the unsuspected vista that flashes suddenly open as we hurry past—"Your right hand is outstretched" recalls Israel's escape through the separated sea, where Moses sings: "Your right hand, Lord, is gloriously powerful." (And also: "You stretched out Your right hand; the earth swallowed them." There God's right hand drowns His enemies, but here it rescues the drowning.)

The final declarations of ne'ilah are those prescribed for a dying man (we think again of the closing gap in time). We end the service by stretching out one final moment (metaphorically we are slowing time to a standstill, standing on the brakes)—with a last long, drawn-out blast of the shofar.

Yom Kippur ends; the judgment books close; the separation disappears; the gates shut.

Unless they remain open just a crack until the day known as Hoshana Rabba, toward the end of the festival of Sukkot (which follows Yom Kippur). Only then, according to widespread belief, is our judgment truly "sealed." The rabbis know that the gates must close, but try to hold them open till the last possible moment.

Which suggests two final observations about separations in time and their role in the art of a Jewish life, in the deep microcosm we are assembling layer-by-layer and in the *Torat ha-lev.*

Because time (unlike space) is linear, cutting it suggests that time might first be drawn thin, like a hot iron bar—not snapped in half but gradually drawn so fine that we can see right through, to God on the far side. Perhaps we are separated from God by the fact of time itself, we rushing headlong within time's stream, God perfectly still outside.

Israel's salvation begins at the burning bush, which draws Moses through the wilderness to God's presence. The bush warps space-time like a black hole leading from the old universe to a brand new one. Moses is astounded: "The bush burns with fire, yet the bush is not consumed" (Exodus 3:2). The miracle is not the burning but the *continued* burning. Those dry thorns should have burned to black dust in an instant. But time has been stretched out, stretched thin, and a moment of instantaneous combustion lasts on and on. The burning bush (a midrash says) *is* Judaism—a fire too hot to last, a life too intense to continue, a sacred gap bound to close unless we struggle unceasingly to hold it open.

* * *

As separations in time are central to this microcosmic theme, so are deliberate social separations.

Rabbinic Judaism was created by a group of thinkers called Pharisees—in Hebrew, *p'rushim:* "those who are separate." In Talmudic Hebrew, betrothal is *kiddushin*—sanctification, from the root *kadosh,* meaning "holy" and suggesting (as we have seen) "separate." A betrothed or "sanctified" woman declares herself separate, set apart for her husband.

To separate yourself from the surrounding world—to pull away and go off on your own—is hugely difficult. It is no accident that Jewish history begins with God's command to Abraham, "*lekh l'kha!*"—get going! Turn your back on everything you have known and push off into the wilderness. Imagine what this must have meant in the ancient world, where families ordinarily passed their whole lives together and separation was much like death.

"Go off by yourselves" is a command Jews have found terribly hard to obey even when their lives depended on it. Pulling loose from Germany in the 1930s was just as hard (despite German bestiality) as pulling loose from Egypt (despite Egyptian bestiality) three-and-a-half millennia earlier. Moses predicted that Israel would be reluctant to follow him out of Egypt, and he was right.

To pull yourself away from the society you live in, which shelters you (or ought to) like your blanket in a cold bed, may be the hardest separation of all—like dragging yourself awake in the dead of night. "Man's general way of behaving," Maimonides notes matter-of-factly, "is to be influenced in his opinions and deeds by his neighbors and friends, letting his customs be like the native customs of the country."

But separation governs the Bible's view of how Israel should live among the nations. The years of desert wandering between escaping Egypt and entering Israel were sacred, like the Sabbath: the nation encountered God at Sinai and became a "kingdom of priests and a holy people." When it crossed the Jordan into the Promised Land at last, the event was modeled explicitly on the Exodus out of Egypt. As the tribes crossed into Israel, "The priests, bearers of the ark of God's covenant, stood solidly on dry ground in the midst of the Jordan; all Israel passed on dry ground" (Joshua 3:17).

But it is not only the river that is rolled apart; whole peoples are, too. The Lord "will displace yes *displace* before you the Canaanite, the Hittite, the Hivite, the Perizite, the Girgashite, the Amorite, the Jebusite" (Joshua 3:10). Later, King David wins a victory over the Philistines and makes the metaphor explicit: "God has broken my enemies before me like the breaking of water" (2 Samuel 5:20). "If the Lord had not been for us, let Israel say—if the Lord had not been for us, when men rose against us, then they had swallowed us up live. . . . Then the waters had overwhelmed us, the stream had passed over our souls; then the proud waters had passed over our souls" (Psalms 124:1–5).

The Bible insists on it: Israel was no virgin territory; the land was not empty. Its pagan inhabitants were rolled apart, and the Jews occupied a forced-open gap still wet with an earlier culture. Where in any nation's literature is there a more astonishing passage than Deuteronomy 6:10–12? When God brings you to a promised land of "great good cities that you did not build, houses full of everything good that you did not fill, and hewn cisterns you did not hew, and vineyards and olive-groves that you did not plant, and you eat and are satisfied— watch yourself!—lest you forget the Lord Who brought you out of the land of Egypt."

Here the clearing out of the land is connected explicitly

to the parting of the Red Sea. Later—for its sins, the rabbis taught—Israel would be engulfed by returning pagan peoples just as Egypt was engulfed by returning Red Sea waters. In the words of a lament for the black fast of Tisha b'Av, the darkest day of the ritual year (on which, tradition holds, both the first and second Temples were destroyed): "The sea waves pounded but stood up like a wall—when I left Egypt; the waters overflowed and ran over my head—when I left Jerusalem."[10]

The land of Israel is itself the culmination of a whole series of prodigious acts of sacred, creative separation. Making the holy land required that earth be created (the primeval waters swept apart), man be created (the primeval human separated into male and female), the patriarchs be created (Abraham separated from his idolatrous home and family), the Jewish people be created (the sea waters forced open to make a birth canal), and finally that the holy land itself be prepared by a sweeping apart of its aboriginal inhabitants.

(Idol worship in the Bible is never merely a wrong opinion; it is a force as black and powerful as the primeval waters of chaos. Paganism has been a deadly force throughout history. Remember what happened when state idolatry rose in Soviet Russia, Imperial Japan, and Nazi Germany like bile in humanity's gorge. Tens of millions died, many tortured to death.)

God makes all these separations in the teeth of chaos, nature, death; and each can be undone. Even the separation between male and female can be undone, in a sense; canceling it has been postmodernism's most deadly dangerous project. As for the separation that created the world, the Lord says (according to the Talmud) that "If Israel will accept the Torah well and good; otherwise, I shall reduce the universe to chaos again."

Recall Othello's cruelly prophetic outburst. "And when I love thee not, chaos is come again."

Three different but related crises in Jewish history illustrate this subtheme (or translucent layer) of social separation:

Moses knew that the Jews would resist being separated from Egypt. They suffered there, but Egypt was their home. "My Lord," Moses says, "why did You send me?" After they have escaped to the wilderness, the Israelites complain to Moses: "Weren't there graves enough in Egypt, that you had to take us to die in the desert? What is this you have done to us, bringing us out of Egypt?" (Exodus 14:11). In the Torah's vivid prose you can hear their voices, and ours.

After the Nazis took over in 1933 and before war started in 1939, it was hard but not quite impossible for a Jew to leave Germany. Some tore themselves away. Others did not. It was not only a matter of Nazi-created obstacles. German Jews were required to take the enormously painful step of separating themselves from their native worlds, ripping themselves loose.

American Jews today are asked to endorse a vastly smaller, easier act of separation, when they are asked to disapprove of their sons and daughters marrying Gentiles. (Who asks them? In an age with virtually no concept of authority, religious life becomes more hit-and-miss all the time.) Increasingly, American Jews refuse. "*Be separate!*" says the midrash; otherwise Judaism ceases. But it's not so easy. The waters want desperately to close.

We can broaden and deepen this historical discussion. Judaism calls on Jews to be separate; anti-Semitic neighbors have often forced them to be separate. Clearly the traditional separation between Jew and Gentile was a collaborative effort. Historically the Gentile swaggered, the Jew lay low. But even before the ghetto there was the cave. The cave foretold the ghetto.

The second century teacher and patriot Rabbi Shimon bar (or "ben") Yohai withdrew from society and lived in a cave for some twelve years. He had to. He had spoken against Rome, and the Romans had (true to form) sentenced him to death. The Romans as usual were murdering Jews by the thousands, often torturing them to death by crucifixion. (Crucifixion is ancient Rome's most characteristic contribution to world history.) But eventually Rabbi Shimon's sentence was lifted or forgotten, and he returned to society.

One result of his long withdrawal, according to the Talmud, was a huge increase in his mental powers.

Naturally. Life in a cave is a life of sensory deprivation; sensory deprivation leads to vivid imagining. Ghetto life partly explains the unique passion, force, and intensity of Jewish culture. Not for nothing does the Zohar put its most important thoughts in the mouth of Rabbi Shimon bar Yohai.

The Zohar is a vast mystical treatise composed by Moses de Leon in Spain at the end of the thirteenth century. It holds a unique place in post-Talmudic literary history. The Zohar became the central text of a school of thought called kabbalah, which originated in Provence and Catalonia in the late twelfth century; it "gained a place in the national consciousness as a canonical text third only to the Bible and Talmud" (in the words of Isaiah Tishby, student of the celebrated scholar Gershom Scholem).

The portentous, sometimes obscure Zohar has attracted nuts and quacks for generations. Nowadays New Agers are gathered round. But the Zohar is a deeply important and serious work. It is a strange and fantastically vivid stream of consciousness, the product (writes the scholar Arthur Green) of "a poetic imagination so extraordinary that any attempt to account for it, either by the author himself or by his readers, seems to lead beyond theories of poetics and toward some form of prophecy or revelation." Maybe that is why it seemed natural to attribute the Zohar to Rabbi Shimon bar Yohai— celebrated as the man who, a millennium earlier, had lived long years in a cave. Persecution and withdrawal lead to the dark cave, where you see little and imagine much; and then to the dreamlike profusion of the Zohar.[11]

Shimon bar Yohai is a microcosm of Judaism all by himself. Sensory deprivation (to varying degrees) has been Judaism's strategy for three millennia. The ultimate philosophical and artistic outcome of "separation" is Jewish theology, and the *Torat ha-lev*. In pursuit of holiness, Judaism starved its appetite for pictures of God (forbidden by the Ten Commandments); starved its need for companionship with neighboring peoples; starved its hunger for normality and its natural longing to blend in and be separate no longer. From the destruction of the second Jewish state in 70 C.E. until its gradual reemergence into the bright light of Western civilization, starting slowly in the seventeenth century, the Jewish nation lived in Rav Shimon's cave and its imagination ran wild.

It would be wrong to overstate the degree of isolation. Influence flowed steadily across the Jewish-Gentile boundary, in both directions. The same Gentile nations that viciously persecuted the Jews drew on Jewish thought for many of their fundamental ideas and inspirations. Western civilization is (among other things) a fantasy on the theme of Judaism.

Yet the cave was just as real as the *Torat ha-lev* (although neither is easy to see at first glance). No nation was ever so scattered as the Jews; none was ever so coherent. Their enemies forced the Jews into a cave, as Rabbi Shimon's had; but at the same time, the Jews *chose* to be inside because they despised their enemies—as Rabbi Shimon did. Israel, said the Gentile seer Balaam, "is indeed a people that will dwell alone, and will not be reckoned among the nations" (Numbers 23:9). When the threat diminished and the Jews staggered out into daylight, their pent-up power (like Rabbi Shimon's) was astounding. They emerged ravenous, with their thoughts racing.

The full story of Jewish achievement in modern art and science has yet to be told. More astounding still is what happened earlier, inside, when the whole genius of the Jewish people focused on the philosophy, poetry, and practice of Torah. Because of this long confinement, the Jews' intellectual history has the strange and glittering and (sometimes) near-delirious intensity of a communal dream. The best word for what they accomplished in exile—scattered and apart and alone—is *zohar*. This Hebrew word of Aramaic origin means "dazzling splendor."

Thus Moses de Leon's story about the authorship of the Zohar is false historically but true artistically. "In a vision I will make Myself known to him; in a dream I will speak to him" (Numbers 12:6). The Zohar says: "A dream needs a good interpretation." Every style of thought has its place in a spectrum of possibilities, ranging from highly focused analytic thought at one end to the richer, more complex, more enigmatic possibilities of dream-thought at the other.[12] Judaism's sacred literature is epitomized by the Bible, the Talmud, and the Zohar; all three tend to be closer than nearly anything else in Western literature to the "dream-thought" end of the spectrum. And the *Torat ha-lev* is thought itself, straight-up.

I have mentioned the central role of imagery in the Bible, and the dreamlike character of the Zohar; many books have

commented on the "stream-of-consciousness" quality of Talmudic and midrashic literature.[13] As the Red Sea escape resonates with Creation, with the lifting of the Torah and with
certain synagogue façades, so the cave of Rabbi Shimon resonates with the command to "be separate," with the history of
Jewish ghetto life and the dreamlike character of Jewish sacred
literature. Thus the rich resonant beauty of the *Torat ha-lev*,
which is constantly disclosing unexpected deep vistas. I will return to Rav Shimon's cave at the close of this book.

Separation in Judaism has profound religious meaning. But
ours is a scientific age. So what does this theme-image tell us, in
the end, about human life and the point of human existence?

The world three thousand years ago included theists and
atheists; so does the world today. Science hasn't changed the
equation. Many of today's scientists are nonbelievers, and
would have been had they lived three millennia ago. But no religious man has ever been made irreligious by science.

In recent decades, some thinkers have tried to use science
to support religion. Fair enough. But the way to do it is not (to
choose one example) by misinterpreting the Bible's creation
story, which is designed to teach about God and man, not
about physics and cosmology. Mere scientific facts are of no
interest to the Torah.

The way to use science on behalf of religion is to put scientific truth to work in writing a commentary on religion's
deep, sometimes puzzling assertions. Thus we have separation,
a basic theme-image of Judaism and of the Torah-of-the-
Heart; an emergent theme to which the Bible and the rabbis
return obsessively. We try to understand its power. What makes
this theme-image so effective? Thermodynamics can help explain.

The rabbis did not anticipate thermodynamics and couldn't have cared less about the topic—but they and the Bible saw intuitively what modern science has measured and codified. They saw and felt that the universe runs down. "Entropy" increases. Entropy is chaos, disorder, mixed-upness. In physical systems, it can be measured precisely. The famous Second Law of Thermodynamics tells us that nature works inexorably to disperse, to eliminate distinctions, to bring all things up or down to the same level. The rabbis saw it all, intuitively. Two thousand years ago they understood it better than most people understand it today.

But they are opposed to the Second Law.

In human society (where physics enters only by analogy), a people disperses—mixes with other peoples and gets lost like a teardrop in the ocean. But Judaism is against dispersion. "He will gather you together again, from all the nations where the Lord your God has scattered you. If your outcasts are at the very rim of the sky, the Lord your God will gather you thence; thence will He take you" (Deuteronomy 30:3–4).

Every organism dies; its physical stuff disperses and rejoins the earth. The Torah and the rabbis know this, but they are against death. Of course death is *natural,* but Judaism is against nature, too. It is against entropy. It opposes the inevitable unraveling of the universe. "Today I call heaven and earth to witness—life and death have I laid out before you, the blessing and the curse; choose life and live, you and your children!" (Deuteronomy 30:19). Colossal words.

The rabbis see the dangers in the inevitable rising tide of chaos in the universe. (But they do not believe in "inevitable.") They have always seen the danger that Judaism will vanish as kosher mixes with *treif,* holidays with normal days, Sabbath with the rest of the week; as Jews "return to nature" and become worshippers of the earth or sky or ecosystem; as they marry Gentiles, do as Gentiles do, and sink back (with a well-earned sigh of relief) into the muddy ocean of mankind.

"It is very hard to drive out pagan spirits," the scholar and historian Shalom Spiegel notes coolly, "and each generation must renew the battle against them."

The rabbis have always understood that the opposite of sanctity is unseparateness. That is what makes the Red Sea escape the defining version of sacred separation; and makes separation, in turn, halakha's central theme. With the Egyptians chasing them and the terrible power of the split-open sea pressing in from both sides, a frightened line of Jews keeps chaos at bay, interposing their own bodies between two terrifying walls of water. When they are gone, chaos returns with a shattering roar. Mankind is broken and overwhelmed. Sanctity vanishes like a hole in the sea.

Although separation is in some ways a slippery and subtle and elusive theme, in the end there is no way to miss it. The public life of Judaism centers on the synagogue, and synagogue worship centers on opening and closing the holy ark. This is Judaism's heartbeat. When the ark is open, we see holiness in the tangible form of the sacred scrolls. Whenever it opens, it is bound to close again.

After we open the ark on the Sabbath and festivals, and before we remove a scroll and open it, we sing words from the Zohar: "May it be Your will to open my heart to the Torah." (The ark opens; the mind opens.) We read from the Torah; then display the scroll held high, wide open; then we roll it closed. Having replaced it in the ark, we repeat a prayer from the end of Lamentations: "Make us return to You, Lord, and we *will* return!"—as if we wanted to squeeze through the ark's closing doors and disappear into a different universe. "Make

our days new again, as of old!"—as if we wanted not merely to
stretch time thin or break it in two but to run it backward,
from age to youth, scattered to gathered, broken to whole,
death to birth. Judaism stands not for acceptance but for
defiance. The ark closes.

We can restate the Second Law indirectly by saying that
time can run only one way; the Second Law is sometimes
called "Time's Arrow."[14] It follows that the prayer we repeat before the ark closes is deeply rooted in Jewish thought. By making separations and creating sanctity, we push hard against
chaos and (in so doing) we push against time itself. Time cannot run backward; yet Judaism struggles, by creating sanctity,
to put you (in a sense) back in your early childhood—when
your vision was large, you could sense worlds you could not
see, and God's presence was as vivid as sunlight on spring
leaves. But just as we know that time is irreversible, we know
that to revisit or reconstruct past time is worthless unless we
retain our sense of present reality. Hence the strange phrase
"Make our days new, as they used to be," or "make our lives
new again." We can't go back in time, but Judaism makes our
past as vividly present as the sunlit sea bottom when we look
downward through clear water.

The Jewish nation believes itself to be God's messenger;
believes its presence on earth to be God's presence, holding the
chaotic waters back. It is an arrogant belief and a humbling one,
and is nearly impossible to bear. Jews are forbidden to pray for
the one thing they want most: to be like everybody else.

"Happy are Israel!" says the Zohar, for "the Holy One
Blessed be He has separated them from all other nations." Israel's arrogance, its greatness, and its noble defiance are all
present in that one word, happy.

* * *

I now return to our starting point, and summarize the answers to the questions with which this chapter began.

> Why does Judaism have such intricate ceremonies and laws? Why can't religion be treated as a personal matter between man and God, with no complex rule book butting in?

To live by halakha means to use ritual acts of separation to create sanctity, and thereby make life into one continuous act of sanctification. Sanctity requires separation: between man and the beast inside; between our high aspirations and our animal nature. Halakha embodies man's defiance of the Second Law of Thermodynamics, in its physical and social shape. Raised on the foundational imagery of birth and creation, halakha says "Choose life" in every law, every word, every letter. It embodies symbolically the Jew's defiance of chaos and death; his absolute refusal to "rejoin nature" and slide back into the meaningless sea of animal existence.

Some halakhic acts of sacred separation are eloquent. Others seem mute and inexplicable. But arbitrary separations, like those of kashrut or the laws of *kilayim,* have their own particular significance. They make it clear that *man* creates holiness by an act of will in the service of God. Even if you merely refuse to eat meat and milk together because such mixtures aren't kosher, your one simple act—with the massed chorus of Jewish law and experience behind it—is a symbolic defiance of chaos, corruption, and death; of the whole process of unraveling to which the natural universe is doomed. By focusing the mind on details, by making it impossible to float through life without paying attention, and by making every moment an occasion for sanctity, halakha reweaves the raveled fabric of humanity. ("How else but in custom and in ceremony," Yeats asks, "are innocence and beauty born?")

Of course, random man-made acts of separation have no such significance. Sorting your books into big ones and small ones or your apples into red versus yellow creates no sanctity. Why not? For those within the practicing community, it is sufficient to answer: "because these separations are not called for in Jewish law or tradition." But there is a broader reason: because halakha is a law of separation that is also intended to create a powerful connection, between each Jew and the Jewish people. If you keep kosher, keep Shabbat and the holidays, say blessings, study Torah, and follow the rest of this intricate and beautiful way of life, you *are* separate perforce from the world at large—and you have twined the thread of your own life into the stout rope of Jewish history, which ties one end of human time to the other.

The Jews stand onstage alone; but, they say to their God with supreme pain and pride, "You are one and Your name is one, and who is like Your people Israel, a nation unique in all the earth?" (from the Shabbat afternoon prayers). To join this nation you must take up the thread of halakha, separate yourself at least in part from the world, and draw close to your God and His people.

# III
# Veil

How can a Jew understand and deal with a God as abstract and indescribable as the unique God of Judaism?

Doesn't this pure and deep but difficult view doom Judaism to be a cold, abstruse, forbidding religion in which man and God stand on opposite sides of an impermeable barrier or infinite gap?

These questions have been nearly as popular among Judaism's Christian antagonists as those in the previous chapter. In recent years, non-observant Jews have posed them as well. These too are good and important questions, whoever is doing the asking. The answers emerge from the microcosmic image-theme I've called "veil."

We looked first at separation—or, in other words, holiness: pulling against nature's current, choosing life. But when we consider God Himself, we face a problem or even paradox.

How do we reconcile these two verses from the same chapter of Exodus? "No man can see Me and live" (Exodus

33:30); "the Lord spoke to Moses face to face, as a man speaks to his neighbor" (Exodus 33:11). This biblical riddle (other verses say similar things) shows us something crucial about the nature of Judaism and the Bible.

To put the paradox in broader terms: God is transcendent and holy, separate from the world He created. ("Let the soul praise God," says a midrash, "Who is exalted above the world, and Whose place nobody knows.") Yet God is intimately accessible: "near to all who call upon Him in truth" (Psalms 145:18). God said to Moses, according to a midrash, that "in every place where you find a trace of the feet of man, there am I before you."

How can transcendence and intimate nearness coexist? How can we imagine God beyond space and time, in an utterly different order of existence from man's, and also imagine Him close at hand?

The solution to this problem (to the riddle and the paradox) is an image. Imagine God and man face to face but separated by a veil.

There is the answer: easy to picture, but far-reaching in its implications. Not an image of physical reality but a hint about God's reality. If God and man face each other with a veil in between, they are face to face yet not face to face. The veil allows transcendence and intimacy to coexist. It hides God's presence but not His nearness.

The far side of the veil is always hidden. We can picture the man and the veil, but not the other side. Picture yourself facing a vast blank. A vertical plane, perhaps of cloth, cuts off your view—you can't see around or through it. But you can approach as close as you like. You can touch the cloth, even kiss it. You can imagine folding it backward or forward. You can picture the veil enfolding or encompassing you, with God's transcendent presence all around you on every side. Or you can imagine it crumpling forward, allowing you to hold a veiled object in your hand.

Separation is a mere physical act; but we saw in the previous chapter that Judaism loads it with meaning. A veil is only a physical object but (again) it is loaded with significance in the Torah of the Heart. It suggests a wedding veil: the prophets imagine God and Israel as married lovers. (Married lovers are the basis of another theme, discussed in the next chapter.) The Torah scroll itself is the most important veil of all.

A veil is no mere opaque sheet; what makes it a veil is the something that is behind or beyond it. In Judaism's veil image, that "something" is transcendent divinity. If a veil, let's say of metal, separates or protects you from heat, you can't feel the heat directly—but the metal heats up and you feel it indirectly. The symbolic or metaphoric veil of the *Torat ha-lev* acts the same way, transmitting an intuition of the Lord's presence, or an inkling, premonition, shudder.

Wherever you move through the universe, the sacred veil (like sheer rustling satin, barely present) surrounds and enfolds you: God's "hands" cupped around you. On its far side is the Lord pure and simple. You move through the universe surrounded by God.

Since the veil is a metaphor, we must make its imagined physical realization true to the underlying thought, and insist on the veil's two basic properties: sheerness and blankness.

It's as sheer and unsubstantial as we can imagine it—a sheet of gold leaf, perhaps, beaten out finer and finer until mere quiet breathing makes it crinkle and flutter. The sheer veil shows us that God is wholly separate yet intimately near, right before us, all around us—yet "real" in a way that is wholly different from our "real," in a realm completely separate from ours. The veil shows us that God will never mix with human beings as a man among men; a rent in the veil tears the very idea of transcendence to pieces. With the veil torn (for however short a time), the two realms mix and become one, and the idea of transcendence is gone forever. Once again, sanctity requires separation.

And the veil is opaque and blank. Its blankness simultaneously invites us to imagine and warns us not to—or, at any rate, not to misunderstand what we imagine. We never decorate the veil with images of God. Any image we can draw is false. Yet its blankness makes our imaginations work, as any blank sheet must. And yet again, its blankness warns us that we can know what God wants and what He offers, but not what God is.[1]

If the veil stands everywhere right before us as the sheerest partition between God and ourselves, we are entitled to see all nature as a veil with God's presence just on the other side. God is not *in* nature but He is just beyond it; *through* nature we feel His presence. Every man is a veil too—although human beings alone are at liberty to choose their degree of (metaphorical) translucence. You can allow the world to feel God's being through you, or you can draw the curtain. The degree of your own religious faith has no direct connection with your choice; we can feel God's reality in the presence of a godly atheist. If *you* are an atheist, you yourself might (nonetheless) be some other person's best evidence that God exists.

Yet, among the small number of persons I know whom I can honestly call "good," nearly (though not quite) all are religious believers.

God is transcendent and imperceptible. Yet the barest of margins, the thinnest of tissues—the mere thickness of a tallit, no more—a "prayer shawl," a sheet of cloth!—separates

man and God. "Whither shall I flee from Thy presence? If I as-
cend into heaven, Thou art there! If I make my bed in the
abyss, Thou art there; if I soar on the wings of the dawn, and
dwell in the uttermost sea, even there shall Thy hand lead me,
and Thy right hand guide me" (Psalms 139; the German
philosopher Johan Gottfried Herder [1744–1803] cites this as
"my favorite psalm," "my morning prayer," and adds: "Can you
name to me such a hymn as this?"). The veil image doesn't say
so, it shows so.

The veil is always near, right before us and surrounding
us. But the tallit reminds us that the veil is no mere partition
between ourselves and transcendence. It is a shawl, too, which
we gather round our shoulders when we need comfort or a
sense of connection to the long continuum of Jewish history.
Enfolding ourselves in the veil is the spiritual analog of enfolding ourselves in a shawl; but God's very presence is what
we gather round our shoulders.

What act do we perform in order to accomplish this
"gathering around our shoulders" of a spiritual or metaphysical veil? The act of prayer. The text of the prayer book is itself
a veil. On its surface it consists mainly of blessings that we pronounce on God and His creation, and blessings that we ask
God to grant us. But when we pray, we do not expect miracles;
the purpose of prayer is not to deliver a daily list of action
items to the Almighty. Its real purpose is to gather round us the
shawl (or veil) of God's presence, and be comforted.

We read this purpose in biblical texts that are part of the
liturgy. "Comfort ye, comfort ye my people, saith your God"
(Isaiah 40:1). "As one whom his mother comforteth, so will I
comfort you" (Isaiah 66:13). "Weeping may tarry for the night,
but joy cometh in the morning" (Psalms 30:5). "They that sow
in tears shall reap in joy" (Psalms 126:5). Above all, in the

twenty-third Psalm: "Yea, though I walk through the valley of the shadow of death, I will fear no evil: for Thou art with me."

The prayer book itself repeatedly refers to God in such phrases as *Av ha-Rahamim*, "father of mercies," "merciful father"; a phrase I have already mentioned, "spread over us *sukkat shlomekha*, the shelter of Your peace," is best understood as a prayer that the shawl of God's presence be gathered round our shoulders—or (still better) as an acknowledgment that, by the act of praying, we have accomplished what we ask. The shelter of God's peace—the shawl of God's presence—is in fact gathered around our shoulders to comfort us.

I have been describing the microcosmic theme itself, but if we want it to live in our minds, we must construct the theme layer by layer, image by translucent image. Like our other themes, the veil image in all its subtlety and depth can exist only in the mind.

Repeatedly we find Jewish literary language that shows us "hidden but close," "set apart yet near at hand," "close yet inaccessible"—and explicitly "curtained off," "veiled," "enfolded." In Jewish sacred literature, screens of all kinds—cloth and leather and stone—separate us just barely from transcendent sanctity. All these images suggest a sacred veil that screens man from God (Who is transcendent) and connects him to God (Who is as close as a groom to his bride).

Like an enormous piano that is struck and then allowed to hum on, the image of the veil resonates throughout Judaism. Nothing is more characteristic of the *Torat ha-lev* and the sacred art object we call a Jewish life than this insistence on a God who is utterly transcendent *and* intimately linked to every moment of existence.

Several embodiments of Jewish faith, seemingly unrelated, are united by the emergent image of the veil. (No one of them suggests the sacred veil on its own, but "superimposed" all together they do.) Judaism does not go in for mysteries, yet each is mysterious.

*The mezuzah:* usually a small case holding a rolled-up parchment sheet. Specified Torah verses are written on one side of the sheet and a three-letter name for God (beginning with the Hebrew letter *shin*) on the other. The case is fixed slantwise to a doorframe. A traditional case, usually of wood or metal, has a small window to let you see God's name on the back of the rolled-up sheet within.

The mezuzah is based on a biblical injunction to write God's word "on the doorposts (*mezuzot*) of your house" (Deuteronomy 6:9). An early mezuzah was discovered at Qumran near the site of the Dead Sea Scrolls. Instructions in the Talmud gave the mezuzah its normative shape. New practices evolved over the centuries. Some (writing God's name on the parchment's back, for example) were accepted; others rejected.

The mezuzah's purpose is explained in the Torah: to make Jews contemplate God's word. The inscribed biblical verses must be written perfectly. Maimonides spells out the location of each ornamental pen stroke. But why does the text turn its back to us? (Why is it rolled with the biblical verses facing in?) If pondering God's words is the point, we ought to be able to read them; why has it become traditional to hide the text in a case that screens it from view—except for one word on the back?

You might object that the text has not been "hidden" but merely rolled up and stored in a suitable container. You might say the same about the "hidden" text inside the tefillin—the black leather boxes men wear at morning prayers. But this is a main characteristic of the emergent themes of *Torat ha-lev:*

they reflect back on the elements that created them. They make us see each in a new way. Once we may have seen only a text inside a container. Now we see (at least for purposes of discussion) a text that is hidden.

*The Western Wall in Jerusalem:* Judaism's holiest site, which once helped support the gigantic, built-up platform of the Temple Mount. But it wasn't always Judaism's holiest site. Until the late fifteenth century the Mount of Olives ranked higher—which seems reasonable, because you have a commanding view of the whole Temple Mount from the Mount of Olives. The Western Wall, on the other hand, is at the bottom of a valley. It has no openings or windows, and when you stand right in front of it you have a commanding view of nothing.

Holy or not, a great ruined wall of huge undecorated stones should be (you would think) forbidding. But worshippers often stand as close as they can get. You see them leaning their foreheads against the wall and, sometimes, kissing the stones. We take this scene for granted. But it is strange (or at least unexpected) to find such tenderness focused on an empty screen; a blank page.

The next two translucent layers are more abstract; yet both add to the veil image when we think about them.

*The carefully prepared horn, usually a ram's horn, called a shofar:* The *shofar* is sounded during the month leading to New Year, on New Year's day (Rosh ha-Shanah), and on the Day of Atonement (Yom Kippur).

The shofar speaks no words and plays no tune. The rabbis describe it as "wailing," "moaning," "crying out." Judaism is a highly articulate religion; distinctly a musical one also. Why should it focus such intense concentration on this inarticulate and unmusical yet humanlike sound? On this wordless, tuneless crying out?

*Finally, God's unsayable proper name,* which is blanked out on purpose. This four-letter word (the "tetragrammaton") occurs throughout the Bible—though less and less frequently in the last of the Bible's three divisions, called *Ketuvim,* or "Writings."

Originally the name was pronounced as it is written. (Like many other Hebrew texts, ancient biblical fragments and rabbinic manuscripts use consonants exclusively. But the vowels can be inferred.) Later it came to be pronounced only during Yom Kippur services at the restored Second Temple in Jerusalem. Later still, after the loss of the Second Temple in 70 C.E., it was no longer pronounced at all. When observant Jews see the name today, they substitute—if they are praying—a generic word for God. If they are not praying, they do not even go that far. They say only *Ha-Shem,* the Name.

The Name is another aspect of Judaism we take for granted—and is one more layer in a deep emergent image.

The dominant note in Israel's relationship to God is love. Hence the Torah's central verse, inscribed on the mezuzah's inner parchment: "You shall love the Lord your God with all your heart, with all your soul, and with all your might" (Deuteronomy 6:5). What does "with all your might" mean? "The idea is to love Him enormously, with everything you are capable of, with perfect love in your heart," writes the brilliant medieval commentator Abraham ibn Ezra. The Talmud calls the Torah "a law of love" (Sukkah 49b). (In the eighteenth century the eminent philosopher Edmund Burke wrote, "Before the Christian religion had, as it were, humanized the idea of the Divinity, and brought it somewhat nearer to us, there was very little said of the love of God." Which is grossly false—but countless others have written basically the same thing, and some still believe it.)

Yet ordinarily we want to say out loud the name of a thing we love, not hush it up. Listen to a devout Jew say "*Yerushalayim,*" Jerusalem, while he prays and you will hear love talking. Furthermore, "name" is a word that functions in biblical Hebrew as it does in such English expressions as "make a name for yourself." The Hebrew phrase "men of name" means "men of repute." For a name to be hidden or hushed up has dark overtones.

A man delights in saying his love's name; would choose to "hallow your name to the reverberant hills, / And make the babbling gossip of the air cry out 'Olivia!'"—as the lady's lover (or rather his emissary) puts it in *Twelfth Night.* If Jews love God, why do they refuse to say God's name?

To see the image that emerges when we superimpose these separate elements, we go back to the start and notice a biblical passage that reminds us of (or resonates with) the mezuzah. God says to Moses: "As My glory passes by, I will put you in a cleft of rock, and screen you with My hand and you will see My back; but My face will not be seen" (Exodus 33:22–23). Rashi (the greatest of medieval commentators, 1040–1105) says that God had wrapped Himself in a tallit when Moses, hidden in the cleft, was allowed a glimpse of His glory. Moses could not have seen the Lord Himself; he would have seen a tallit in which the Lord was (somehow) wrapped.

That tallit would have been a literal veil or "sacred screen" between God and man. The traditional mezuzah has evolved into a symbolic picture of that awe-striking scene: "I will screen you with My hand and you will see My back, but My face will not be seen." The mezuzah lets us see God's name on the parchment's back—but the text on its face remains hidden.

Here is one of Judaism's deepest thoughts, and one of the most important principles of *Torat ha-lev:* the ineffable, transcendent reality of God can be closer to you if it is *hidden* from you—behind a veil or "sacred screen."

"The biblical passages are numerous that tell of the fear and trembling that seizes the prophet at the moment when the Divine Presence *actualizes* itself for him," writes the twentieth century philosopher Eliezer Berkovits. If a man were to find himself literally in God's presence, then "before he could grasp the sight," writes the thirteenth century sage Nahmanides (commenting on Exodus 33:20), "his soul would be gone." Men cannot exist face to face with God.

You cannot see God; you cannot exist in His (unveiled) presence. Yet this transcendent God is no inaccessible, faraway abstraction, as so many casual observers of Judaism have claimed. God is ineffable *and* close at hand. We can approach God exactly when He hides himself; then and only then. And though you cannot see God, you can see the veil—in fact touch it; even kiss it. You can approach the veil with the awe-inspiring knowledge that God, unimaginable and inconceivable, is nonetheless on the other side. This idea of an "uncompromised" God Who is infinite and transcendent yet (still!) near to all who need Him is one of the crowning masterpieces of *Torat ha-lev.*

This "hiddenness" of God is not, of course, what Moses and Isaiah mean when they speak of God's turning away or hiding Himself because of man's unworthiness.[2] On the contrary: this "hiding," or "screening," is what we read about when God tells Moses, "I will screen you with My hand." It protects man from God's presence and symbolizes (at the same time) God's ineffable transcendence. God is outside time, outside space, infinitely vast, infinitely powerful—and the intimate companion of all who need Him.

Judaism was born into a pagan world. A pagan world is "closed"—the gods correspond, ordinarily, to objects that are visible in the sky or sea or landscape, or they might live on top of a mountain, or be present in some species of animal. Judaism opened the top of this closed universe (as the sliding roof plates might creak open in some giant observatory dome), revealing the infinity of transcendence and profoundly, decisively expanding man's intellectual and spiritual universe.

But through this open top there is nothing to be seen that man's eyes can register. (It's easy to picture absolute blackness but impossible to picture nothingness.) So Judaism covers the opening with a sacred veil, which is not God and not an image of God, but *is* the concrete connection human beings need to an idea as abstract and difficult as transcendence—and to a God Who is wholly separate from human beings yet intimately involved in human life.

The sacred veil is as ubiquitous in Judaism as is separation. What does it mean? Let us build the microcosm layer by translucent layer.

The Talmud says that mezuzah, tallit, and tefillin are all connected. "The people Israel are beloved. The Holy One Blessed be He has surrounded them with mitzvot: tefillin on their heads, tefillin on their arms, tsitsit [the knotted fringes at the tallit's corners] on their clothes, mezuzah on their doors" (Menahot 43b). These objects all resonate together. Each sets the others humming. All contribute (when you superimpose them in your mind and think of them all at once) to the emergent image of the sacred veil or screen.

Moses' face shone with light after his contact with God

on Sinai—and thereafter he "veiled" or "screened" it (Exodus 34:33) so as not to scare anyone. The veil reappears as the pair of curtains screening the Holy of Holies in the Temple at Jerusalem, and later as the curtain screening the holy ark in synagogue. In the Zohar, the light of creation and the light shining from Moses' face as he descends Sinai are the same light. Moses wraps himself in that light (says the Zohar) "as in a tallit, as it is written: 'He wraps Himself in light as in a garment'" (Psalms 104:2).

Tallit and mezuzah are intimately related. Looking at a tallit, we see not merely the garment but one version of the emergent theme-image: the unbounded vastness of God separated from finite man not by a complex theological superstructure nor by flocks of angels but by a plain piece of cloth; a sacred veil.

A Jewish male wraps himself in a tallit for prayer every morning. (Some have the custom of wearing the large "tallit gadol" only after they are married.) Many worshippers pull the tallit over their heads when they say the crucial prayer called *sh'-moneh esrei*, the Eighteen Blessings. The Talmud tells us that, to be a legitimate religious act, this prayer must be said in a specific frame of mind: the worshipper must imagine himself in God's presence (Sanhedrin 22a and elsewhere);[3] this prayer is often called the "Amidah," the one that is said "standing," because you stand before God when you recite it. Standing, you imagine that your tallit alone separates you from the Lord; you are Moses in the cleft on Sinai. The sacred screen can be soft as cotton on your face.

In the synagogue ceremony of the priestly blessing (performed every day in Israel, on major festivals elsewhere), each man of priestly descent (each "kohen") covers his face and lifted hands with his tallit. Other congregants avert their eyes as the kohanim chant together: "May the Lord bless you and keep you; may the Lord let His countenance shine upon you and be gracious to you; may the Lord lift up His countenance to you and grant you peace" (Numbers 6:24–26). For a moment each kohen is symbolically lit with the Lord's light and the tallit is—once again—the sacred veil. Notice the pregnant combination of sacred veil and divine "face." When the kohanim chant, "May the Lord let His countenance shine upon you and be gracious to you," their own faces are veiled with the tallit.

Repeatedly Judaism shows us one object or event shattered like a shaft of light by a prism into countless diamond flecks. Moses veils his face after encountering the Lord. Today countless kohanim veil their faces before blessing the people, as if they themselves had just encountered the Lord. A veil creates the presumption of a far side; the veiled faces of the kohanim create a presumed or imagined (recent) past in which each kohen encountered God for himself and departed physically aglow. We can't see the radiance, but the veil makes us imagine it. The veil helps make the infinite Lord real to human minds.

Judaism allows no representations of God; is therefore said by some critics to be "visually impoverished," "abstract," "cold." In fact the *Torat ha-lev* offers representations of God that are richer and more evocative than mere images of humans or quasi-humans. Judaism understands man's hunger for images. But for Jews the mezuzah, tallit, tefillin, and other instances of the sacred veil are "representations" of the Lord—because God's presence lies just on the other side, and we feel that and know it. (But such representations can never be confused with God Himself, or worshipped as idols or totems.)

The man Moses is re-created in the totality of veiled kohanim (past, present, and future) blessing Israel. In the Bible, the famous three-part blessing ("May the Lord bless you and keep you . . .") is spoken originally by the Lord to Moses, with orders that it be conveyed to Aaron and his sons—Israel's first priests. Today no individual kohen (meaning an ordinary Jew whose family traces its descent over millennia to the original caste of priests serving in the Holy Temple) can represent or stand for Aaron, much less Moses. But the sum of *all* kohanim, blessing the whole people throughout Israel's history, do stand for Moses collectively. Shattered and scattered, the brilliant presence of Moses (luminous with knowledge of God) covers the whole space and time of Jewish history with diamond flecks of light.

Consider the sheets of text sealed inside the tefillin (or "phylacteries")—the opaque, near-cubical black leather boxes that a man wears on his forehead and arm during morning prayers. Here a "screen" enfolds the sacred text, and you can hold the veiled object in your hand—a small box that suggests in microcosm the cubical Holy of Holies of the Temple in Jerusalem. (When you hold a tefillin box you hold—in a sense—the Holy of Holies in your palm.) Again, one Holy of Holies becomes countless tefillin throughout the space and time of Israel's history—as one Moses becomes countless ordinary Jews blessing the people.

In the First Temple—King Solomon's, built in the tenth century B.C.E. and destroyed by the Babylonians in 586 B.C.E.—the tablets of the Covenant were kept inside the Ark. The Ark cover was screened by cherubim's wings; the whole Ark was screened off within the Holy of Holies. In most Ashkenazi synagogues today, the ark containing the Torah scrolls has (as I have said) a curtain in front, called the *parokhet*, conceal-ing its doors from view. To remove a Torah scroll we part the curtain and open the ark, then (having passed through a series of screens) remove the scroll. After carrying the scroll or *sefer Torah* to the reading stand, we come face to face with the ac-tual words on parchment. Later I will discuss how the words themselves become a veil—at which point the "far side" of Torah comes alive like a struck match in our imaginations.

Only one thing can penetrate the veil. "The people Israel are beloved," says the Talmud. For the great Israeli storyteller Shmuel Yosef Agnon (who died in 1970), a tallit symbolizes love between God and Israel. "He Himself, in His glory, sits and weaves—strand on strand—a tallit of all grace and all mercy, for the congregation of Israel to deck itself in."

The sacred screen is associated not only with God's tran-scendence but with His love. It separates and connects. It sep-arates God and Israel like groom and bride. Love (love alone) can penetrate the veil. Love converges on the veil from both sides. "I will shield you with My hand," says God to Moses—a protective, loving gesture. Moses is shielded by God's love from God's power. And when we ask (in the words of the prayer book) that God "spread over us the shelter of Your peace," we ask Him to do what He did for Moses: to screen, protect, and shelter us with the veil of His love.

The biblical verses hidden inside the tefillin boxes read, in part: "You shall love the Lord your God with all your heart, with all your soul, and with all your might." The same com-mand is hidden inside the mezuzah. It is customary to kiss the tefillin before putting them on and after removing them. As we finish putting them on, we recite a passage from the book of Hosea (a passage based on a radical and remarkable image that I will discuss further). God tells Israel: "I will betroth you to

Me forever." Some Jews have the custom, when they enter or leave a room, of touching the mezuzah and then kissing the fingers that touched. God is hidden like the mezuzah text, separated from Israel by a sacred screen that is like a bridal veil—opaque except to love.

Another layer in this deepening microcosm: worshippers at the blank Western Wall in Jerusalem believe that God returns their love somehow from beyond or inside. The wall is a perfect physical embodiment of the sacred screen because there is no longer any Temple behind or beyond it. The physical reality of the far side is gone. Imaginary or metaphysical reality has replaced it. For those (Jews and others) who wrongly believe Judaism to be an austere, abstract religion that disdains imagery, the wall is a blank screen marked "Stop! Thou shalt not imagine!" But in fact it says to worshippers, "transcendent sanctity is so near, you can feel it in these stones—as you feel a hidden fire roaring on the far side of an ordinary wall."

A natural progression (just what we expect in the *Torat ha-lev*): the First Temple centered on the Holy of Holies, which held the Ark of the Covenant. That Temple was destroyed. When a Second Temple was built, the Ark was gone and the Holy of Holies was a (supremely evocative) empty space. ("It remained inexplicable and simply amazing to the later Greeks and Romans that there was *nothing to see* at the center of the Jewish Temple.")[4] Then the Second Temple was destroyed. Today Judaism's holiest site is a mere empty envelope, with neither ark nor temple inside. "Nothingness" has spread to the very boundaries of the physical enclosure. Thus we are left with the veil alone, the veil itself—eloquent outcome of two historical catastrophes. But a strange Talmudic passage (Baba Batra 99a) tells us that the space within the Holy of Holies was

undiminished even when the Ark of the Covenant stood inside—as if the Ark had always been absent, from the very first.
As if its eventual disappearance had been foreshadowed by a
strange quirk of physics.

At the wall, you see how a sacred veil can embody Judaism's highest truth. You see also that this blank is no theological abstraction; it draws Jews close.[5] The literary critic
George Steiner (whom I have mentioned earlier) has the idea
that God's ineffable transcendence makes Judaism a pure yet
forbidding religion. Steiner cites the composer Arnold Schoen-
berg's libretto for his opera *Moses and Aaron* (1930–32), in
which Moses is made to proclaim God "Inconceivable because
invisible / because immeasurable; / because everlasting; / because eternal; / because omnipresent; / because omnipotent."
This Mosaic view is "much more authentic, much deeper,"
Steiner writes, than the concrete view held by Moses' brother
Aaron. But Moses' profound conception is "accessible only to
very few"; its "abstraction and inwardness" place it "beyond
the power of ordinary men."

Steiner's view is intriguing—and exactly wrong. The veil
itself, the veil that symbolizes God's inconceivable transcendence *itself* draws man and God close. It is a bridal veil, joining
God and Israel in love.[6]

An articulate, musical people focuses its full attention on a
sound with no words or melody. Sacred occasions culminate
in wordless, tuneless wailing. Why?

The shofar plays an unusual role in synagogue. It is no
bell or bugle issuing a summons; no drum imposing order.
The shofar's sound announces nothing. It itself is announced,
by a sung or spoken formula. And as long as it lasts, it is the
center of attention.

In nearly any synagogue, any sounding of the shofar is a moment of intense collective concentration. Here again (as in the raising high of the Torah), Judaism uses mere physical difficulty to make a spiritual point. The shofar can be a hard instrument to play. The difficulty of sounding it, and the fact that the shofar player sometimes fails, contribute to the intensity of the congregation's attention. The energy curve of the long New Year's morning prayers peaks during the shofar calls.

The shofar makes a direct appeal to God unburdened by words. We have no words with which to describe God or address Him. So how can we address Him? ("The language of the heart is central," writes Ibn Ezra. "The spoken word serves merely as an interpreter between the heart and the listener.")[7] The shofar bypasses language and translates thought and emotion directly into sound. The shofar expresses what words cannot. Practicing Jews will see the relationship between its sound and the end of Shakespeare's *King Lear,* where Lear's loyally loving daughter Cordelia has been hanged and Lear's line is "Howl, howl, howl!" The outer limits of language and the territory beyond are central themes of Shakespeare's greatest play. That territory beyond language is the territory of the shofar—and of the *Torat ha-lev.*

Wittgenstein believed that we cannot reach this territory-beyond-language; language (he taught) is a closed, windowless cell and we are permanently locked inside. "Our words will only express facts, as a teacup will only hold a teacup full of water even if I were to pour a gallon over it." But maybe the shofar's sound lets us slip outside the locked cell for just a moment (like space-walking astronauts).

The rabbis establish the character of the shofar's sound in one of the Talmud's most striking passages (Rosh ha-Shanah 33b). What is the meaning, they ask, of the Hebrew word used by the Bible in connection with the shofar's sound? To explain, they cite the translation of that Hebrew word in the classical Aramaic version of the Torah,[8] and then cite another verse from the Aramaic translation where the same word plainly describes a mother's mournful outcry when she grasps that her warrior son is dead and will never return. So we understand that the shofar's sound must be—is *meant* to be—a mournful outcry.

And amazingly this biblical mother in mourning is none other than Sisera's mother, in the book of Judges—the mother of the Jews' deadly enemy, of the man who "oppressed the children of Israel powerfully for twenty years," and whose death was a joyful deliverance. Sisera's mother, before grasping that her son is dead, had been daydreaming about the great man's (presumed) latest triumph. She had pictured him doling out the spoils: "a woman, two women for each man" (Judges 5:30). And yet Jews when they appeal to God by means of the shofar use *this* woman's voice—the voice of their bitter enemy's foul mother who becomes, in her grief, just a fellow human being. The Torah of the Heart understands mother love as a basic building block of the universe; in this light, all mothers are equal. And the shofar's blast becomes a universal cry for mercy, addressed to the God of all mankind.

A midrash tells us that, on hearing the shofar, God "rises from the seat of justice, and sits on the throne of mercy." In this emergent theme-image of the *Torat ha-lev*, transcendence is associated with God's love. The shofar's humanlike voice seems (almost) to speak—but we can't understand it. In fact the shofar calls, says a midrash, are like a secret code concocted by two lovers (God and Israel) so they can speak privately and shut out the world. The majestic, awe-striking sound of the shofar speaks for all mankind—yet is also a secret love code between God and Israel, who are head over heels. Paradox helps us grasp God's vastness.

Paradox—but let's be clear. No people is closer than Israel to its God. The veil speaks of God's transcendent apartness *and* nearness—God is hidden (as I have said) like the mezuzah text, separated from Israel by a sacred screen like a bridal veil—opaque except to love. I underline this because even today, some—not all—Christian theologians tell us that it is by dint of the Christian liturgy that "the God of the Old Covenant, the tremendous and the distant, comes nearer to his people."[9]

But no God comes nearer to His people than the Jewish God. The veil shows His nearness (not just His transcendence), and there are so many ways to make this point concrete that one hardly knows where to start.

Only Jews argue with God—and keep arguing, as they have done from biblical times to this afternoon; there is no truer sign of closeness. This "arguing" theme has been discussed by so many authors at such length that I feel safe in omitting details here. In the Five Books of Moses, Abraham and Moses have famous arguments with God; the thread continues through the rest of the Bible, through the Talmud—I will discuss an important Talmudic example later—and continues all the way into the early modern period in the lives of important Hasidic *rebbes* and then into the Jewish literature of our own day.

Or: ponder a male Jew's words every morning (except Shabbat) as he finishes binding on his tefillin, those holy-of-holies in microcosm, the black boxes with Torah verses inside that he will wear while reciting his morning prayers. He speaks lines from the prophet Hosea, *God's* lines—but he repeats them to himself, like a lover repeating His beloved's endear-

ments. "I will betroth you to me forever." And then, "I will betroth you to me in righteousness and justice, in kindness and
compassion." And then, "I will betroth you to me in faithful-
ness—and you will know the Lord" (Hosea 2:21–22). God's
love, says Hosea, is as desperate and enormous as a gale at
sea—and as fathomless and incomprehensible as a parent's; in
any case, God is near.

You can sing without words; can you speak without them? A
sacred veil is a blank. Even if it is decorated, as a tallit gadol
may be, by its nature it blocks our view. Accordingly this veil
theme encompasses layers of blankness, of emptiness, of seeming meaninglessness. We must continue stacking translucent
layer upon layer, and see what emerges when we look into the
depths. Gershom Scholem, the celebrated historian of Jewish
mysticism, reports a "highly remarkable" statement by the
nineteenth century Hasidic rabbi Mendel of Rymanov. When
God spoke to all Israel at the foot of Sinai, the people heard
only the very first letter of the first word of the Ten Commandments—the letter *aleph* that begins the word *Anokhi*, a
stately way of saying "I." Whereupon they were overwhelmed,
and Moses stepped in to mediate and be a screen between God
and Israel.

The remarkable fact is, Scholem notes, that the letter
aleph represents virtually nothing at all. Merely the position
taken by the larynx when a word begins with a vowel. In everyday terms, the aleph is a silent letter. To hear the letter aleph is
to hear essentially nothing. The Israelites were overwhelmed,
according to Rabbi Mendel, not by the sound but merely by the
*approach* of the Lord's voice. God's presence is overwhelming
even if you cannot see or hear it, even if you (merely) know it
is there.

The divine presence makes itself felt through any veil. And the veil itself—represented by tallit, t'fillin, mezuzah, and many other symbols—takes Moses' place between God and Israel.

The people hear God once, at Sinai (or, according to Rabbi Mendel, they *almost* hear Him once), and resolve never to do it again: "Do not let God speak to us, lest we die" (Exodus 20: 16). Familiarity is the opposite of what they want; they want protection from God's presence. God says, "I will favor whom I will favor; I will pity whom I will pity" (Exodus 33:19). In short, I will do what I want. Moses tells the Lord, "They will say to me, what is His name?" God answers: "I am Who I am. . . . Say: 'I Am' sent me to you." In other words, you won't know who I am, only what I say.

And therefore when practicing Jews see God's proper name, they say something else. They disregard the sounds (or voices) of the letters (in Hebrew, "sound" and "voice" are one word), because those letters spell the holiest word there is. They place this name outside language—as the shofar's sound comes from outside, through a window on darkness. They place this name outside the sacred veil. Its four letters no longer reveal its sound; now they are only a screen to hide its sound.

Those four characters screen the name's sound behind a blank like the Western Wall; hide it in a black box like the tefillin case. Rabbi Shimon bar Yohai held that God's names—the tetragrammaton and all generic words for God—were literally enclosed (or hidden) within the Ark of the Covenant (Baba Batra 14b). Some opinions hold that the Ark's contents rested inside an ark inside an ark inside an ark: three layers of sacred veil (Yoma 72b).

Some embodiments of the veil image (or layers within
the veil microcosm) are physical: Moses' veil; the curtains before the holy ark in synagogue and the Holy of Holies; mezuzah, tallit, teffilin; the Western Wall. Some are symbolic: the
shofar's sound, God's voiceless name. There is even a prescription for making the Torah itself the most important veil of
all—by dissolving its meaning.

God cannot be "made beautiful"—the idea is blasphemous;
but the things of Judaism and especially the sacred veil's symbols *can* be beautified. "This is my God and I will adorn him"
(Exodus 15:2). "Rabbi Ishmael said," according to a midrash,
"can a man beautify the Creator? [No], but I will make myself
beautiful to Him through the commandments . . . beautiful
tsitsit, beautiful tefillin . . . or Torah scrolls; I will write the
scrolls for His sake with beautiful ink and a beautiful pen by the
hands of practiced scribes, and wrap them in beautiful silk."

The prescription for making a sacred veil of the Torah
comes from a figure I have already referred to in this chapter:
Nahmanides—Rabbi Moses ben Nahman, "the Ramban," who
was born in the Catalonian town of Gerona in 1194. His formi-
dable commentary on the Torah brings the whole rabbinic tradition to bear, word by word, in a hugely detailed discussion.
(In modern Hebrew type, the Ramban's Torah commentary—
albeit with heaps of editorial footnotes throughout—runs to a
thousand-odd pages.) Obviously his goal is to explain the
meaning of every sacred word. Yet he writes in the introduction to his commentary: "the whole entire Torah is *names* of
the Holy One Blessed be He" (my emphasis).

He means that, if you pay no attention to the sense of the
words and change word boundaries freely, sliding letters back
and forth as if they were beads on an abacus, you can read the

whole Torah as a string of names for God (including descriptions of God that can serve as names). This is a kabbalistic doctrine that also appears in the Zohar. It is a method of reading Torah that sets its meaning to zero; that drains all the sense out as deliberately as you pull the plug in a basin of water.

Why? The Ramban gives us an actual method for *not* understanding—a way to reset to zero the plain sense of the sacred text, to flatten it so that every word means the same thing, keeping the letters but erasing their usual meanings; turning the text into a great featureless windblown sand flat where all you can hear (in the wind, or the plunging crash of distant waves) is God and God and God. Yet he himself wrote a thousand pages to explain these same words one by one!

What drove him to press on past understanding? "Isn't he going backwards?" writes Nietzsche (in *Beyond Good and Evil*) about a case something like the Ramban's. Nietzsche answers, "Yes! But you understand him badly if you complain about it. He is going backwards like someone who wants to take a great leap." Exactly. A great leap is just what the Ramban plans.

Notice first that not understanding can be much harder than understanding. Every child learns his native language; but *un*learning it—hearing the word "blue" (say) as pure sound without meaning—is nearly impossible. Yet "unlearning" offers unexpected rewards. The great twentieth century artist Alberto Giacometti once described, as a central event in his life, a moment at which the people around him suddenly stopped seeming like people and became (for a moment) unrecognizable. Only when these most familiar of all objects became strange was he able to see and grasp them properly for the first time.

To "achieve meaninglessness" seems like a negative goal. But in the case of the *Torat ha-lev,* it reflects no desire to diminish (let alone bypass) the words of the text. Instead it captures the conviction that there is more to the text than just its sense. The extra ingredient is holiness. And you can see sanctity better when you blank out the distraction of meaning—as you can see the sun's glowing halo (its "corona") only when a solar eclipse has blacked out the main disk. Usually the corona is invisible.

Of course there is no value to meaninglessness per se, or to meaninglessness in some random text—just as there is no value in random acts of separation. But the Torah is no random text. Each generation has been told by the previous one that these are God's words. The chain of tradition—a chain of voices, of parental murmurings—connects each one of us directly to Sinai. The goal of a Jewish life is to be part of a live connection (an "open circuit") from the revelation at Sinai all the way forward to the coming of the messiah.

God gave the Torah "potential" holiness, gave Israel the chance to *make* it holy. (Thus Rabbi Joseph Dov Soloveitchik: "Holiness is created by man, by flesh and blood.") And Israel responded to this gift. "A man should not say," according to the Talmud, "I will study so they will call me wise, I will learn so they will call me rabbi, I will study to be an elder with a seat in the yeshiva. Instead, study out of love!" (Nedarim 62a). Thousands of years of love and devotion have made the Torah a radiant body. You can see and feel this radiance best when the glare of human meaning has been dimmed.

Jews have loved the words of Torah for a long time—not just the words but the letters, their exact shapes. Once you have gotten beyond the meaning of words, you can see the Torah not as a text but as a beloved face. These letters are, collectively, a beloved face. And faces don't "mean" anything.

By reading the Torah in a way that blanks out the sense,

the Ramban associates himself with the most esoteric type of mysticism—and also makes the plainest, simplest kind of assertion. He acknowledges that the face of Torah is holy, and lovely, for its own sake. He goes the law and tradition one better; he "beautifies a mitzvah." Every Jew must study Torah not for practical gain but *li'shma,* for its own sake. That is a mitzvah. Better still, the Ramban seems to suggest, study the actual letters of Torah (not just the words!) for their own sakes. Don't stop at the meanings of words; ponder the beauty of each letter.

Jews want to understand Torah but also to pass right *through* meaning and keep going. In the *Torat ha-lev* the text becomes more than a text; it becomes a veil too, with transcendence beyond. How does the transformation from text to veil take place? By dint of not understanding. To understand the words of Torah—a lifelong effort—moves us closer to God. To understand and then move past understanding takes us even closer.

The transformation from meaningful text to meaningless screen brings the far side into imaginative existence.[10] Suppose there is a fence or gate right in front of your nose. The gate is decorated with wrought-iron letters. You can focus on those letters and read them—in which case the scene beyond is a blur. Or you can peer *through* the gate, between the letters—in which case the letters (inches from your face) are a blur. Reading the gate blurs the region beyond; focusing on that region beyond blurs the letters.

This simple thought experiment hints at how a text can "lose its meaning"—and acquire in that very process the imaginative possibility of a far side.

Consider several related "texts": God's name (once pronounced, now letters that mark a silence); the Torah's words (not only a text but a sequence of God's names); the calls of the shofar (a humanlike voice that we can't quite make out). What image emerges from all these phenomena? What do we see when we overlay all these translucent images?

The sacred veil.

In studying conflicting opinions in the Talmud, the rule is: these *and* those are words of the living God (Eruvin 13b). The Talmud is built out of argument and controversy. Of 523 chapters in the Mishnah, only six have no disputed points. Most disputes are resolved—but hundreds are not. And almost all views (accepted and rejected) are preserved and must be studied. One view is accepted in practice, but every view has something to teach us about sanctity and God's will.

Contradictions are the essence of Talmud. You can't look at a page without running into them. Begin with paragraph one on page one of volume one, *Berakhot,* "Blessings": "Starting when do we say the evening *sh'ma* ['Hear, O Israel . . .']? From the hour when the priests enter [their homes] to eat their *terumah* until the end of the first watch—according to Rav Eliezer. But the sages say: until midnight. Rabban Gamliel says: until the dawn rises." Three different answers to one simple question.

The Talmud is built out of contradictions and clashing rabbinic disputes like a skyscraper out of steel beams at right angles. Religious law must, in the end, follow one view and reject the others. But Jews must study them all, with the knowledge that "these *and* those are the words of the living God." How do we account for the ever-present contradictions, and their role as building blocks of Talmud?

These ubiquitous contradictions "de-focus" the Talmud much as the Ramban de-focuses the Torah. When a north-traveling wave runs into a southerly one they might both be

*Shma.* The Hebrew "*Shma*" ("hear!") is the first word of the short
confession of faith recited daily, both morning and evening: "Hear, Israel!
The Lord is our God; the Lord is one" (Deuteronomy 6:4). This is also the
last statement of one who is dying—directed not to God in supplication
but to the nation and the future in proud affirmation.
(Collection of Susan and Roger Hertog)

*Ha'Mavdil.* The Hebrew phrase "Who separates [*Ha'Mavdil*] between sacred and ordinary" is taken from the blessing that marks the transition from sacred to ordinary time; it praises God as the "separator," thus the creator of sacred time and of sanctity. (Collection of the artist)

*Ha'Azinu.* The Hebrew phrase "Let the heavens hear [*Ha'azinu*] and I will speak" begins Moses' last charge to the assembled nation before his death. (Collection of the artist)

*Ein Sof.* "*Ein Sof*" ("Endless," or "Infinite") refers to God in the mystic literature of the Kabbalah—which insists that, in the end, human language has no purchase on transcendent divinity. (Collection of the artist)

*Yishama.* The Hebrew phrase "May there be heard [*Yishama*] in the cities
of Judah and the courtyards of Jerusalem . . ." is taken from the last of
seven blessings in honor of a newly married couple. It continues,
". . . the voice of joy and of gladness; the voice of the bridegroom
and the bride." (Collection of the artist)

*Blue Mezuzah.* The Hebrew phrase in cursive on the pale-yellow strip
beneath the butterfly, "You have learned to know that . . ." (Deuteronomy
4:35), continues, ". . . the Lord is God; there is none else but Him." This
is the first of a series of verse read aloud before the *hakafos* or parade-of-
the-Torah-scrolls on the festival of *Simchas Torah.* The large green Hebrew
letter *shin* suggests the *shin* on the mezuzah and on the *shel-rosh* ("to be
worn on the forehead") of a pair of *t'fillin* or phylacteries.
(Collection of the artist)

*Echad.* The Hebrew phrase "A unique nation in all the world
[*Goy echad ba'aretz*]" is from afternoon prayers on Shabbat;
the phrase reads in its entirety, "You are one and Your name is
one—and who is like Your people Israel, a unique nation in all
the world?" The liturgy insists with sadness and pride on Israel's
unique responsibilities to the Lord and to mankind. The leaf-
border in orange running beneath the letters is patterned on
Gothic masonry (Exeter Cathedral, probably late fourteenth
century) and suggests a series of burning-bush figures.
(Collection of Susan and Roger Hertog)

*Hadeish Yameinu.* The Hebrew phrase "Make our lives new again [*Hadeish Yameinu*], as they used to be" (Lamentations 5:21), is the last phrase we say after replacing the Torah scroll and closing the ark. (Collection of Susan and Roger Hertog)

annihilated, leaving the surface calm. The Talmud's contradictions show that all "meaning" is only human meaning. God's
transcendent truth cannot possibly be captured in human
words. So we think as hard as we can, try our best to grasp the
Talmud's reasoning and its sense, embody our conclusions in
practical guides to halakha ("*halakha l'ma'aseh*")—and then
let the sense spill like dry sand through our fingers.

The letter, spirit, and meaning of the law (every word of
it) remain essential. The religious law is a score that turns lives
into sacred symphonies.[11] But no human mind can encompass God.

The opposing voices in the Talmud accomplish something else,
too. The Talmud's aesthetic and literary qualities are a grossly
neglected topic. Yet this text at its best is tersely powerful and
speaks in short, memorable jabs. And the constant back and
forth of Talmudic argument yields a texture that recalls the antiphonal voice against voice of classical Hebrew poetry. The
Talmud is not poetry and has none of the formal parallelism
that marks classical Hebrew verse. But the echoing back-and-
forthness of Talmudic argument reminds us of the Bible.

Biblical poetry is "prose poetry" by definition, without
rhythm or rhyme. In fact, it is the greatest prose poetry the Western world has ever seen; it sets a standard that has never been approached. "Could you ever discover anything sublime in our
sense of the term in the classical Greek literature?" Coleridge
asked. "Sublimity is Hebrew by birth."[12] At its very best, the Talmud rises nearly to the literary heights of the Hebrew Bible.

Indeed the whole sacred literature of Judaism is full of
antiphonal voices, contradictory opinions abolishing each
other like waves approaching from opposite directions, canceling each other out. The disagreements are important, the

law is essential—and human limitations hover always in the background. A yeshiva where the Talmud is studied today is full of those same antiphonal voices, discussing, arguing, and explaining, in the characteristic yeshiva chant. (Anyone who has ever heard the "Four Questions" sung in traditional style at a Passover seder knows the character of this chant.)

The Talmud has always been studied aloud, and chanted. The Hebrew and Aramaic text has virtually no punctuation. The chant takes the place of punctuation, and clarifies the structure of the unfolding argument. With the printed page bringing the words and the reader supplying punctuation, the reader becomes (once again) part of the text.

At a yeshiva you can be part of a class or discussion or dispute. Or you can close your eyes and let the arguing and counterarguing wash over you. This seemingly meaningless sound is the furthest thing from mere noise; it is built of meaning, it presupposes understanding. But it goes beyond, past understanding, toward the outside of the universe. This might be the nearest a Jew can get to hearing transcendence or seeing its gleam in the crack under the door. "This round world has nothing to rest on," says a medieval Talmud commentator, "but the breath of Torah study from the mouths of students."

God's transcendent presence creates a murmur of sanctity in the universe. That murmur is what you hear in a yeshiva when you can no longer distinguish the words.

When someone dies and we say the memorial prayer, "Lord full of mercy," we meet another of those simple but fathomless phrases that capture the pure pitches of Judaism and the cosmos. We ask that God grant the departed "perfect peace *tahat kanfei ha-shekhinah*," beneath the wings of God's presence. We ask that the departed be gathered to God's side beyond the veil.

The phrase recalls cherubim's wings screening the Ark of the Covenant, curtains screening the Holy of Holies, Moses' veil, God's own hand protecting Moses, the *sukkah* of God's peace sheltering Israel; or the blanket spread by parents over a sleeping child on a cold night. Judaism has developed many doctrines about death over the millennia, but the simplest and deepest is this: our dead are beyond the veil—which is opaque, inviolable, and impenetrable, except by love.

The idea of God's transcendence (or utter separateness) is part of the Bible. It was first developed as a formal concept by the Alexandrian Jewish philosopher Philo at the start of the first century C.E. The contemporary scholar Daniel Matt has traced this idea of "the unknowability and indescribability of God" from Philo through Maimonides in the twelfth century, from early mysticism through classical Kabbalah into Hasidism. But if you are looking for the clearest embodiment not of the ineffable but of *intimacy* with the ineffable, of closeness to the indescribable divine, of the *Torat ha-lev* in action, you will find it in the practices of (for example) certain Hasidic communities.

Gathered in their study-and-prayer houses on Saturday evenings, these groups of Hasidim often push past the end of Shabbat into a ritual called *melaveh malkah*—accompanying the (departing) Sabbath queen. She is the metaphorical embodiment of Shabbat peace; she is traditionally associated with the Shekhinah, God's sheltering presence.

Singing goes on into the night, and at first the songs have words. But after a while the singers tend to shake the words off and continue in meaningless syllables. These are men whose lives are disciplined by an intricate legal code; who work hard to search out the meanings of their sacred texts. But now they want to pass through meaning and come out the far side, as they have passed through nightfall and the end of Shabbat and emerged—not into the next week, but into a state of suspension (perhaps equal in its pregnant ambiguity to the space between the two curtains—like two doors one after the other—that screened the Holy of Holies). When you push past the edge of Shabbat, you might find yourself in a spiritually uncharted realm of sanctity. Singing in a dark room, these Hasidim are back in the cave where Rabbi Shimon bar Yohai passed twelve years hiding from the Romans; where the imagination soars unthinkably.

Meaning parts like a curtain, and the bare human voice reaches outward toward God. If they can understand but transcend the meaning of their holy books and emerge on the far side, they will come face-to-face, *panim el panim,* with the Torah itself (not the mere letters but their physical shapes) and they will hear the actual voice of Torah (not the words but their physical sounds), and this face and voice that they love, not for their meanings but for themselves, as you love a man or woman—this face and voice of Torah are the beloved face and voice of God's own people. *Amkha,* they call it, *Your* people—the mothers and martyrs, heroes and fathers, scholars and children, and our own departed beyond the veil.

In Judaism we seek not just the meaning but the face and voice of Torah, as we seek the face and voice of our dearest love. What could a face possibly "mean"? Nothing: we love it for itself. Everything: "Let me see your face, let me hear your voice; for your voice is sweet, and your face is beautiful" (Song of Songs 2:14).

Again we return to the beginning of the chapter and its questions:

How can a Jew understand and deal with a God as abstract and indescribable as the unique God of Judaism? Doesn't this pure and deep but difficult view doom Judaism to be a cold, abstruse, forbidding religion in which man and God stand on opposite sides of an impermeable barrier or infinite gap?

The answer, in summary: Judaism's God is indeed a unique being outside time and space, Who never has and never will assume human form; Who is literally indescribable. The God of Judaism is indeed "Inconceivable because invisible; / because immeasurable; / because everlasting; / because eternal; / because omnipresent; / because omnipotent."

And yet Jews invented the Hebrew phrase "Our father Who art in heaven" to address this ineffable God. They feel close to their God. Not always; sometimes it is an awful struggle to locate God and feel His presence; sometimes it is impossible. Yet the sacred veil makes it possible for Jews to move close to their "inconceivable" God. They cannot see Him or know Him, or speak to Him face to face; but they can move as close as they choose to an embodiment of the veil—to the tallit that enfolds them, or the Western Wall, or the curtains before the holy ark, or the Torah scroll itself—and in so doing know and feel that God is just on the other side.

The sacred veil means that man and God can *be* and yet *not be* face-to-face. And even though the veil is opaque, is a blank (like the indecipherable words of the shofar), one thing *can* get through, namely, love: man's for God, God's for man. The veil is blank, but is warm with the radiance of God's presence and care and love, and with the presence of our own beloved dead who are gathered "beneath the wings of the Shekhinah"—just on the other side.

# IV
# Perfect Asymmetry

Isn't normative or Orthodox Judaism inherently anti-woman, insofar as its public ceremonies are conducted by males? Assuming we reject the idea that women are in any way inferior, aren't we forced to make basic changes in Judaism?

In more positive terms: how does Judaism understand sexuality, the family, and relationships between man and woman?

These questions lead to some of Judaism's most important aspects: its striking definition of man, its view of the home as (in major respects) successor to the Temple, and its idea of human sexuality as a force that holds the spiritual universe together.

"Separation" and "the veil" are easily pictured. (Of course, they are not just images but microcosms; all of Judaism is present in each.) But in this chapter and the next, the image that emerges from many translucent layers is unfamiliar. I call this chapter's image "perfect asymmetry," which occurs when two differently formed parts are put together to make a perfect whole: black and white keys on a piano, ultramarine and cool red in a rich purple, the wick and the flame in a lit Shabbat candle. In Judaism the two preeminently unlike parts of a perfect whole are (naturally) male and female human beings— but also "maleness" and "femaleness" in general. More surprising is the perfect whole they make. Added together, one male and one female equals one man, one human being.

To construct this microcosm we must turn from the intellectual to the sensual side of Judaism: to the cult at its core, and at the core of the *Torat ha-lev*. "Cult" has a pagan ring, but it need not. It might suggest the sacrificial cult at the ancient Temple in Jerusalem, but that is not what I mean, either. I mean religious ceremonial, centering less on words than on acts, in an environment separated (at least for a while) from daily life. Ritual purity plays a part. Sacred food and drink usually play a part. There is always a certain poetic density in a cult, and a sense in which the main actor is symbolically transformed into something more than human. The Friday-evening ceremony welcoming the Sabbath at home is a cultic event.

In any religious system, cult is the sensual component. In Judaism, "sensual" is underlined. Judaism encourages a heightened sensitivity (in the way some people are always aware of the sun, clouds, prevailing winds, taste of the air)— not to nature but to man. Judaism focuses, moreover, not on the next life but on this one; and not on saints and angels but on plain human beings.

In this spirit the rabbis of the Talmud contemplate an ancient love poem, a poetic dialogue with male and female voices alternating. Not just any love poem; an explosively ecstatic, overflowing song in which the vividness and occasional stumbling-forward awkwardness of the imagery create an air of breathless hurry—the power of speaking left far behind by the power of wanting: a striking erotic effect. The rabbis considered: should this poem be included in the Hebrew Bible? By the way, it never once mentions God.

Rabbi Akiba (I have cited him before) is the greatest figure in the Talmud. Here is his opinion of this poem: God forbid that anyone should question its sanctity. (The actual phrase he uses, *has v'shalom,* will be familiar to anyone who has ever heard Yiddish-flavored English.) Given Akiba's authority, his view decided the question. And today you can open any Bible and read this masterpiece of erotic folk-poetry, the Song of Songs. (Christian Bibles call it the Song of Solomon.)

In common with other ancient and medieval rabbis, and in keeping with the famous image in Hosea I have already mentioned, Rabbi Akiba interpreted the Song of Songs as a duet between God-the-lover and Israel-the-beloved. But he said something else that is even more striking than his powerful endorsement of the Song's sanctity, something that might qualify as the most startling comment ever recorded about this or any other biblical book: "The whole world put together is not worth the day on which the Song of Songs was given to Israel."

We cannot understand Judaism or the *Torat ha-lev* unless we understand how these words echo through it.[1] The rabbis are vividly attuned (like a painter to the nuances of his pigments) to the male and female aspects of everything in the universe. Jewish thought is steeped not in sex but in sexuality—in maleness, femaleness, and the power between them, the power of universal human gravitation. (Again, science offers us metaphors that can help focus and clarify our thinking.) The Bible speaks with extraordinary depth and truth on this topic. And then the rabbis, building on explicit hints in the Bible, color the whole spiritual cosmos in male and female shades.

The literature and thought of the last century happen to be obsessed with sexuality—thanks in part to secular Jewish writers and thinkers. This obsession is not incongruous with Judaism. But it is out of balance; it shows how things can come unglued when we banish cult and sanctity. And the ugly heart's desire of many contemporary thinkers—that marriage should (in effect) be deconsecrated and collapse into the background noise as just one more "arrangement" among many—is indeed un-Jewish. (In parts of Europe it is already a done deal. "Today . . . only the lower orders and what remains of the gentry bother to marry, and everyone else takes a partner, as if life were a dance, or a business venture" [John Banville, *The Sea* (2006)].) Likewise the idea that manliness should disappear, except maybe as a template for girls, and womanliness for boys. Likewise the idea that the sexes should become interchangeable and then melt together, thereby discharging the battery that operates civilization—wiring its two poles together, shorting humanity out. All these ideas are profoundly un-Jewish, not to say inhuman.

Before we investigate this theme-image, a word on a topic the rabbis rarely discussed or felt any need to deliberate: homosexuality. Nowadays the issue has moved near the top of our ethical, social, and political agenda, and no community is free to ignore it; none can avoid pondering it.

Biblical Judaism has nothing to say about homosexuality as a state of mind or personality trait or "orientation"; those are strictly modern terms. The Bible does recognize that some people engage in homosexual practices, and condemns those practices unequivocally[2] (Leviticus 18:22; 20:13).

But there are other principles to be considered as well. A powerful theme in rabbinic Judaism urges that all Jews be treated as one family—"*haverim kol Yisrael*," "all Jews are comrades," says the prayer book, paraphrasing a biblical verse. A phrase from the Psalms (133:1), "*hinei ma tov u'ma na'im, shevet ahim gam yahad*"—"here is what is good and satisfying: dwelling as brothers, united"—is one of the Bible's best-known passages, and the lyric of a perpetually popular Israeli song. Historically, no national or religious community has ever shown a stronger impulse to gather in and embrace all its members, no matter who or what they are, than the Jewish community. This holds true today for all branches of Judaism, and every synagogue worthy of the name.

Many rabbinic passages make clear that God accepts us for who we are. So long as we try to move toward Him, it is the upward or inward struggle that counts, not the point of arrival. One remarkable and moving midrash describes a son who has abandoned his father and regrets it—but in some respects (we infer) is unable to change: "His friends said to him, return to your father. He said, I cannot. Then his father sent to say: return as far as you can, and I will come to you the rest of the way. So God says, *return to me, and I will return to you.*" God's statement means "come as far as you can; I will love you for that."

None of this alters the truth that, in normative Judaism, homosexual behavior (not "homosexuality" per se) is a grave sin. In religious terms this fact is grounded not in bigotry nor even—entirely—in the all-important biblical commands to "be fruitful and multiply" and to "choose life!" (If couples don't reproduce, communities die.) When we trace the rabbinic view down to the ground, as I try to do in this chapter, we find (maybe surprisingly) that it is founded on something else: the essential role of the female in human life, and the "perfect asymmetry" of God's creation.

Nonetheless, the Torah is man's to interpret; the rabbis have made important changes before. (One of the most famous is the rabbinic decree that outlawed polygamy, which the Bible of course allows.) Will normative Judaism's attitude to homosexual behavior change, too? Urged on by the gay rights movement, homosexuals seeking such change have made their presence felt in every branch of Judaism, including Orthodoxy.

*Will* attitudes toward homosexual behavior shift within normative Judaism? That depends on the Orthodox community as a whole and on its *poskim*—the rabbis who rule on normative practice era by era, day by day. What we know for sure is that the community will visit and revisit this issue in the future, and that "*haverim kol Yisrael*" will never disappear from the prayer book, or from the minds and hearts of observant Jews.

Finally, a broader issue. Nowadays American homosexuals (and members of other aggrieved groups) are unlikely to be persecuted. They are more apt to be unhappy insofar as they are unable to win positions they want, positions that are available to members of other groups. This sort of thinking hides the fact that nearly all of us wish (sometimes desperately) for qualities or attributes (leading to jobs, status, or many other possibilities) that we don't have and never will. How do we react to the uncomfortable discovery that other people have things we want but will always be denied, through no fault of our own? I will return to this point.

The cult at the core of Judaism is dedicated to the God of Israel, but is in fact a cult of family—specifically, of the married couple. It is a proper cult, with sacred ceremonies, laws of ritual purity, songs, texts; and even, in a special sense, a hereditary priesthood. And it has its own particular sacred occasions. As Passover is (among other things) the center of the cult of family in general, the cult of the couple in particular centers on the Sabbath. On Shabbat, the married couple is exalted as God's culminating masterpiece (or the man-made culmination of God's creation). God's presence flares up between wife and husband. The main actress is (poetically) transformed.

The cult of the couple and the family has shaped Jewish life for two millennia at least. It is built on human reality: not on an idealized view of marriage but on the facts of prenuptial agreements and divorce. Nonetheless, it has given the Jewish family a unique stability and centrality, exalted the family cult's "priesthood," and given marriage—ordinary human marriage —a supreme importance wholly unlike its status in any other of the great religions Judaism has fathered. It has fostered no mere respect or reverence for marriage; it has gone much further than that. It has reshaped, refashioned, bent, and twisted the whole spiritual universe around the married couple—as molten glass is reshaped by the glassmaker; as space-time is bent and twisted by the gravity of a giant star.

Perfect asymmetry is an image that suggests (or is associated with) a certain idea: a force field between maleness and femaleness that creates marriage and is so powerful it reshapes the cosmos. Bearing in mind that the "sacred woman" in Judaism is never the virgin, always the bride, and that the bride's voice permeates Israel, we can build this microcosmic theme layer by layer.

Start with the Bible. Its writing on relations between male and female is a supreme achievement of realism and beauty. But you must be tuned to the biblical frequency or you will miss it.

One aspect of the Bible's realism is unvarnished grim truth. Sarah, unable to conceive, tells her husband Abraham to sleep with her maid. He does. The girl gets pregnant and lords it over Sarah, who blames Abraham. Sarah is mad at her husband, mad at the maid, and (no doubt) mad at herself. She lashes out at Abraham: "The Lord judge between me and you!" In his short reply—"Look, the maid is in your hands; do what you want with her" (we can picture him turning and walking away)—we hear repugnance, guilt, and a husband's desire to wash his hands (in this case almost literally) of sexual consequences.

More grim sexual truth: Michal, daughter of King Saul and wife to his successor David, speaks to her husband after he has "danced before the Lord with all his might." She is near-jubilant with superior disdain for his vulgar and peasantlike (as she sees it) behavior: "The king of Israel has really covered himself with glory today!" He hits back in the way that will hurt her most: "Before the Lord, Who chose *me* over your father . . . I will be even grosser than that—with the servant girls!" Later, David's son Amnon, lusting for his half-sister Tamar, overpowers and rapes her. And then he despises her, for now "he hated her with hatred even greater than the love with which he had loved her."[3] The most famous verses in the Song of Songs are these (8:6): "Love is strong as death, jealousy is cruel as the grave: the coals thereof are coals of fire, which hath a most vehement flame." Truths that cut to the bone.

But sexual reality is hardly all bleak. There is, for instance, sex appeal, frankly acknowledged. (Reflections on the beauty of the human body were hardly a Greek monopoly in ancient times.) David: "ruddy, with beautiful eyes and good looks" (1 Samuel 16:12). Absalom: "In all Israel there was none to be praised so much for his beauty; from the sole of his foot even to the crown of his head there was no blemish in him" (2 Samuel 14:25). Rachel: "beautiful figure, beautiful appearance" (Genesis 29:17). David admires the unclothed Batsheva ("Bathsheba" in the Authorized English Version): "From up on the roof he saw a woman bathing, and the woman was good-looking; very" (2 Samuel 11:2). The king's palace in Jerusalem was on a hill, with the town sloping away,[4] and no doubt Batsheva was gracefully seated or on her knees behind the parapet, as she languidly poured water ("languid" is Batsheva's middle name) over her moonlit body. Was she pondering the king on high, as he watched her with those "beautiful eyes"?

That scene has a kind of echo in a rabbinic comment on a verse in the book of Esther. Seven days into a noisy royal party in the Persian capital, the king (his heart "merry with wine") commands his courtiers "to bring Vashti the queen before the king with the crown royal, to show the people and the princes her beauty: for she was fair to look on" (Esther 1:10–12). But she refuses to come. The rabbis explain why. When the king ordered her to appear wearing the crown royal, he meant *only* the crown royal.

At times the Bible is explicit, notably in the Song of Songs: "Open to me my sister, my love, my dove, my undefiled" (5:2). But equally significant are passages where the sex is implicit. "Avimelech king of Philistines looked out his window and saw: there was Isaac playing with [or 'laughing with' or 'teasing' or 'flirting with'] Rebecca his wife" (Genesis 26:8; the verb is a pun on the name Isaac, which is built on the same consonants as "playing with").

Romantic ardor: Jacob labors seven years to win Rachel, but "they seemed like just a few days to him in his love for her." (And then he has to work seven years more before he finally gets her.)

A sustained, flirtatious come-on: the first encounter between beautiful Abigail and David. Abigail's husband is a rural powerbroker who has been rude to David's gang. She intercedes, "falling on her face before David," "bowing to the ground," "falling at his feet." "Upon me myself, my lord, be the

offense," she says—"may your maidservant whisper to you?—
would you hear the words of your maidservant?" "Please forgive your maidservant's transgressions."

Maidservant, maidservant, maidservant—which might
also be translated (even better!) "slave girl." Of course this is
standard operating procedure in addressing an oriental poten-
tate. But David at this point is king of nothing; he is the outlaw head of a ragged criminal band on the run. Naturally he
falls for it. He eats it up. "The Lord be blessed!" he says. "And
blessed be your good sense, and blessed be *you!*" (1 Samuel 25:
23–33). Ten days later, Abigail's husband happens to die. "The
Lord smote him," reports the Bible, maintaining its usual
straight face. "Blessed be the Lord!" proclaims David, and invites her to join his entourage, and she gladly accepts.

Sometimes the text upends our expectations. In classical
antiquity, only friendships between men are supposed to be
interesting. But the most famous friendship in the Bible, edg-
ing out even David and Jonathan's, is Ruth and Naomi's.
("Whither thou goest I will go, and where thou lodgest I will
lodge; thy people shall be my people and thy God, my God";
Ruth 1:16. This miraculous "recursive antiphon," a poem in
half a verse, has two balanced parts each made of two balanced
parts, each made in turn of two balanced parts; eight parts in
all. "Whither thou goest": "I will go," and so on.) Or again: a
woman in antiquity was valued first and foremost as a maker
of babies.[5] But when Hannah is bitter at her childlessness, her
husband comforts her (1 Samuel 1:8): "Why should you cry,
and why should you not eat, and why should your heart grieve?
Am I not better to you than ten sons?"

Teasing, bantering, and romance might seem like small things,
taken for granted. But in fact such things as teasing (Isaac and

Rebecca), bantering (Abigail and David), and romance (Jacob
and Rachel) are huge. Along with tenderness (Hannah and her
husband), they are the acts and emotions that turn sex from an
animal into a human proposition. Because it accomplishes the
extraordinary feat of humanizing sex, the Bible makes it possible to use sexual electricity to light up the cult of family like
a dazzling paradise.

The whole structure of the biblical family, as of all Western families until modern times, put the wife in the husband's
power. He acquired her and took her home. In Hebrew as
in many other languages, the feminine form of "man" (*iysh*)
means "woman" (*ishah*). *Ishah* is presumably derived from
*iysh* as "woman" is presumably derived from "man." And the
story of Adam and Eve—Adam is created first, then Eve is
"built" from Adam's rib (Genesis 2:22)—is a physical embodiment of this linguistic relationship, language made flesh.
(There is far less distance between word and thing in the Bible
than in modern language. "Word" and "thing" translate to the
same Hebrew word—or thing.) Just as the word "woman" is
derived from the word "man," the actual woman is "derived"
from the actual man. "She shall be called woman," Adam says,
"because she was taken out of man" (Genesis 2:23). (Words can
act like images, and show rather than tell us about reality.)

But here is the very next verse: "Therefore shall a man
leave his father and his mother, and shall cleave unto his wife."
We are used to this sentence, but its first hearers must have
been stunned. "A *man* shall leave"? Traditionally the groom is
a free agent but the bride is transferred from her family's protective domain straight into her husband's. Thus, for example,
the Book of Common Prayer: "Who giveth this woman to be
married to this man?" What followed ordinarily was the symbolic transfer of the bride from her father's to her new hus-

band's household. But the Hebrew verse seems to turn the tradition upside down.

And consider God's reason for creating Eve in the first
place. The Lord says (Genesis 2:18), "It is no good man's being
alone"—five words in Hebrew, arguably the most perfect sentence ever composed. The prophet Hosea, referring to the Lord
Himself as Israel's husband, sets out the biblical ideal of marriage: a husband will no longer be his wife's lord and master
but rather her man, as she is his woman. "On that day it will
come about, proclaims the Lord, that you will call me 'my man'
[or 'husband'] and no longer call me 'my lord' [or 'master']"
(Hosea 2:16). What could the ancient world have made of that?
(There has been much scholarly discussion of the second half
of Genesis 2:18 also: God says of Adam that "I will make him a
helper *k'negdo.*" The Hebrew word means, in essence, "over
and against him." The English "helpmeet" descends from the
King James translation of this phrase ["I will make him a help
meet for him"], and suggests that Eve is intended not as a sub-
ordinate but as a partner. Some modern discussions take Everett Fox's translation[6] as a starting point: "I will make him a
helper corresponding to him.")

As recently as the first half of the twentieth century,
American wives (albeit wryly or snidely) used the phrase "my
lord and master" to mean "my husband." And many could
dimly remember (or thought they could) a society in which
"my lord and master" was not invariably a joke.[7] So there is an
implicit warning in Hosea's words: if we try to apply to ancient
Judaism or to the Torah of the Heart-and-Mind the academic
categories of our own day—"patriarchal," "matriarchal," "feminist," "anti-feminist"—we are guaranteed to go wrong. Jewish
thought is profoundly out of synch with the rest of the world,
sometimes by around 2,500 years.

One other notable aspect of the Bible: although wit and humor (generally dry and underplayed) crop up in many passages, women are more likely than men to sound witty, detached, or ironic. Accordingly they sometimes seem more modern than biblical menfolk. Possibly this ironic detachment reflects unhappiness in a male-dominated society. Possibly it doesn't. At any rate, it is plain that the Bible observes female characters at least as carefully as it does males.

At one end of the spectrum we find broad, good-humored, female-perpetrated mockery. Jacob's favorite wife, Rachel, for example, steals her father's family idols. When he confronts her she says, "Let not my lord be angry with me that I am unable to rise before you, but I am in the female way" (Genesis 31:35). She's hidden the idols and is sitting on them. (You can hear the bystanders giggle and snicker.) But there is no amusement in Sarah's famous laughter: the Lord or an angel has promised Abraham a son by Sarah—but they are both old, "and Sarah laughed to herself." The divine visitor admonishes her for laughing. She denies it "because she was afraid," but the visitor says, quietly, "No. You did laugh" (Genesis 18:12–15). The utter realism of this little conversation gives it a strange, compelling majesty. I have mentioned Michal's disdainful sarcasm when she confronts her husband like a princess addressing a peasant. No literature knows its characters better than the Bible, women emphatically included.

The redefinition of man that puts sexuality at the center of the universe is an outgrowth of the admiration for women that is typical—although not universal!—among the rabbis of the Talmud. (Furthermore the Bible is almost never sentimental, but the rabbis sometimes are.) The cult of the married couple begins in the Talmud, based on explicit hints in the Bible. The

Sabbath as its feast day is another Talmudic idea, one that gains definition over the centuries and bursts into fragrant bloom in medieval and postmedieval mysticism.

"Whoever has no wife," says the Talmud, "lives without joy, without blessing, without goodness." A midrash ups the ante: a man with no wife "lives without goodness, without help, without joy, without blessing, without God's forgiveness." Biblical verses are adduced to support each of these assertions. (This process of repetition-with-elaboration is typical of rabbinic literature.) Rabbi Shimon adds, "indeed without peace," and gives a biblical prooftext. Rabbi Joshua adds, "indeed without life," with another prooftext. Rabbi Hiyya adds, "indeed such a man is not whole," and gives still another. (This hints at the direction in which our emergent theme is moving.)

"Some say that such a man degrades the very archetype of God," the midrash continues, "for it is said, 'in the image of God He made man.' And what follows right after [in the text of Genesis]? 'And you shall be fruitful and multiply.'" In other words: man cannot *be* "God's image" unless he is prepared to "be fruitful and multiply"—unless he is part of a couple; unless he has a wife.

By now the topic has changed. From wife-praising the rabbis have turned to a different, fundamental subject: what is man? They are preparing a surprising answer.

The Hebrew *adam* means "man," usually in the sense of "human being" rather than "male." It is also the name Adam. But the Zohar adds a new meaning. Citing the verse "Male and female He created them . . . and He called their name man" (Genesis 5:2), it asks, why "their" name and not "his"? And answers: "Anywhere male and female are not found together, the Holy One Blessed Be He does not place His abode there. Blessings are found nowhere but in a place where male and female are found, as it is said: 'He blessed them and called their name Adam on the day they were created.' It is not said, 'He blessed him and called his name Adam,' *for man is not so called except when male and female are one*" (emphasis added).

In Judaism, then, God is one but man is two—not male *or* female but male *and* female. Man and woman must come together not merely so that a child will be born but to create a whole man out of two halves. Whether or not a child is engendered, the sexual union of husband and wife is inherently blessed.

The implications of the Zohar's definition are far-reaching. In sexual union, human beings may not be at their best or noblest, but only then are they complete. Among the most startling implications of the Zohar's view is the idea that a human being is not a creature at all but an event, flickering into existence for a few moments here and there, a shimmer of flame.

Other traditions have stories of male and female uniting to form a whole; Plato mentions one in the *Symposium:* "primeval man was round, his back and sides forming a circle; and he had four hands and four feet, one head with two faces," and so on. Zeus splits these circle-men in half "to humble their pride and improve their manners." Thereafter the two halves long to reunite. The radical differences between this kind of story and the Zohar's view are obvious. There are no primeval grotesques; God creates one male and one female, each physically whole but emotionally and spiritually incomplete. In the Zohar's view, human beings themselves have the task of creating man. God creates only the raw materials.

Man's nature is more truthfully captured by the Zohar than by tiresome biology buffs who love explaining that human beings are mere animals and nothing special. "If a man and his wife are worthy," says the Talmud, "the Shekhinah," God's presence, "rests between them." Rashi explains: male, *iysh*, is spelled *i-y-sh;* female, *ishah,* is spelled *i-sh-h.* "Male" has a *y* that "female" lacks. "Female" has an *h* that "male" lacks. Together, *y* and *h* spell God. (Once again letters, like images, can show the truth and not merely tell it.)

When the rabbis repeat these stories about words and letters, they are not playing games. They are studying reality indirectly, the way you might study a photograph. As a photo is a two-dimensional image of reality, language in Judaism is reality's shadow, the image of a higher-dimensional world. And biblical language is the shadow of divine reality.

The cult of the married couple as conceived by the rabbis assumes that maleness and femaleness are perfectly asymmetric. Perfect asymmetry describes male and female as they relate to each other sexually. It describes (ideally) mother and father as they rear children. And it also describes male and female roles in society.

Occasionally we find biblical women shining in fields that are ordinarily masculine: Huldah the prophetess, Deborah the military leader. (The story of Deborah's victory centers on women—Yaël, who kills the Canaanite general Sisera, Sisera's mother, Deborah herself.) Ezekiel angrily denounces bad male *and* bad female prophets. Much later, long after the destruction of the First Temple in 586 B.C.E., Ezra numbers female as well as male singers among the host returning to Jerusalem and Judah from captivity in Babylon.

In the Bible's view, male and female are (furthermore) equally interested in sex. Ordinarily the male makes the advances, but not always: Abigail flirts with David before he flirts with her. In the Song of Songs, the girl's desires are just as sexually loaded as her lover's—and she has more lines in the script.

But in general, the rabbis assume that men and women will behave and be treated differently. Their ideas of manliness and womanliness follow from this assumption.

The ideal man is a courageous fighter for God and Israel, for justice and sanctity. Moses enters the biblical narrative by destroying with one stroke an Egyptian who has been tormenting a Jew. It is no accident that the object we associate with Moses is a "staff" or big stick. When the Talmud says, "in a place where there are no men, *you* strive to be a man," we think of Moses striving to transform Israel from rabble to nation.

The best-loved man in Israel's history is King David. As a puny teenager he screams bloodcurdling, near-hysterical defiance at Goliath, the mountainous hit man with his dim, scarred, evil face. Scenting battle, David is transformed; is beside himself with lethal, heaving rage. He is a natural warrior, a fighter of unmatched prowess. Yet he is also remembered as the greatest poet in Hebrew, and perhaps in history. Certainly he is the most influential poet in history. "Thou anointest my head with oil; my cup runneth over. Surely goodness and mercy shall follow me all the days of my life; and I will dwell in the house of the Lord forever." At the very center of English literature we find these sacred words translated from the Hebrew. David is celebrated as the warrior-poet who worships the Lord with joy, dancing before the ark in Jerusalem. The Talmud infers from the Bible that David prayed, too, with desperate intensity (Berachot 30b), going far beyond ordinary bounds (according to Samuel Eliezer Halevi Edeles, the Maharsha). He never could control himself, and Israel condemned and loved him for that.

There are two versions of Judaism's ideal woman. In one

version—in a sense, the official one—she is heroically brisk, efficient, brilliant. This is the view we find in the biblical poem "Woman of Valor" (or, better, "Noble Woman"), which concludes the book of Proverbs (31:10–31). Nowadays husband and family sing it to the lady of the house on Friday night, at the start of Shabbat: "She rises when it is still night; she gives food to her household, orders to her servant girls. She considers a field and buys it. With the fruit of her labor she plants a vineyard. She girds herself with force, and makes her arms strong. . . . She is clothed in strength and beauty; she smiles at the future . . ." But also: "She reaches out to the poor, and extends her hand to the needy. . . . Her mouth is full of wisdom, and the teaching of loving-kindness is on her lips. . . . Her children rise to bless her, her husband to praise her: 'Many daughters do nobly, but you outdo them all.' . . . Acknowledge her achievements! Let her own deeds praise her at the gates." If this biblical exhortation had been let alone (just one among countless notable passages), then "acknowledge her achievements!" would have remained just that—a biblical exhortation. By singing the poem every Sabbath evening, husband and family *do* acknowledge her achievements.[8] This is one element of the cult of the couple.

But the best-loved woman in Judaism is Jacob's wife Rachel, and she is beloved because of what Jeremiah says about her: "A voice is heard in Ramah, lamentation, bitter weeping; Rachel weeping for her children; she refuses to be comforted, because they are not." Because of Rachel's intercession, say the rabbis, the Lord resolved to bring the Jews home from exile, home to Jerusalem.

Such brave, strong, manly heroes as Abraham, Moses, and David argued with God. Rachel did not argue. She demanded and got.

It is striking that both Judaism and Christianity (especially Roman Catholicism) should have elevated a weeping Jewish mother to a central place of honor. That Christianity should have lavished such sublime art over the centuries on images of a Jewish mother grieving over her murdered child is cruelly appropriate, given Christianity's traditional relations with the religion that begot it. Yet the contrast between Rachel and the Virgin Miriam is telling. There is nothing immaculate about Rachel. She is a recognizable human being with many faults, emphatically a bride and a wife—and her husband is in love with her.

Jews do not venerate their heroes and heroines. They love and feel close to them. Throughout history many have felt closer to Rachel than to anyone else except (perhaps) David, and Rachel's tomb outside Bethlehem ranks higher in Jewish minds than any other holy site except the Western Wall.

Ideas about manliness and womanliness are related to, but not quite the same as, ideas about sexual roles. Ordinarily, Judaism puts males in charge of the public, outer world and females in charge of the private inner sanctum. Women may nonetheless take on as much as they want and can get in the outer world—so long as we are talking about the secular world. The religious world is different. It is partitioned, like the Temple. Men are in charge of public religion; women take precedence in private religion at home.

Of these two, the private domain has become the more important. It wasn't always; in ancient Israel, male members of the priestly castes—Kohens and Levites—were born to be ministers in the Holy Temple, and did their main duties within its precincts. The high priest's duties took him to the innermost precinct of all, the Holy of Holies.

When the Temple was destroyed, the synagogue and the home jointly superseded it. And the home is more sacred than the synagogue. We might say that the Temple's outer precinct became (symbolically) the synagogue; the inner sanctum—the Holy of Holies—reemerged as the Jewish home. We will see that the Shekhinah is symbolized by many things, but most powerfully by the woman of the house when she re-creates and embodies the Sabbath.

Although the priestly castes still exist among Jews, and male Kohens and Levites still perform certain rituals, women are the true priesthood of postexilic Judaism. Both husband and wife, for example, are obligated to create light at home on Sabbath evening; but the woman's obligation is stronger, and she fulfills the commandment for the entire household. Even if her husband wants to light the Sabbath candles himself, the woman's claim comes first (according to the *Mishnah Brurah,* an important commentary on Judaism's most authoritative compilation of halakha).

And how do we know that the inner world at home is more important than the outer public world? The Mishnah tells us that Jewish men are, and Jewish women in general are not, obligated to perform positive, time-dependent commandments—for example, to say certain prayers every morning. (Negative commandments—"thou shalt not steal"—bind everyone all the time.) Thus we learn that home duties are more important than the Lord's own positive commandments—insofar as the conflict between them is resolved in favor of the home and against the commandments. (Some authorities excuse Torah students, too, from the positive, time-dependent commandments.)

A male Kohen and a woman are each born to be honored—and in a ritual sense, restricted. (In Judaism the restrictions are always concrete, the rewards metaphysical.) Women, for example, cannot lead public prayer services. The same prohibition applies to a female hazzan, or cantor. In most aspects of synagogue worship, the leader performs the commandment of public prayer on behalf of the congregation. But you cannot perform a commandment on someone else's behalf unless you are obligated to perform it yourself; this is a basic principle of *halakha*. The women in the congregation may, but the men *must*, perform the religious acts associated with public prayer. So a (nonobligated) woman cannot fulfill the commandment on behalf of the (obligated) men.

Some contemporary Orthodox rabbis seek to expand women's public role within traditional Judaism, even to the point of having women lead parts of the public prayer service and participate in reading the Torah.[9] Other scholars and leaders (men and women) disagree.[10] One noted authority, Rabbi Shlomo Riskin, argues that these particular functions are anyway not basic to the rabbinic role, which has traditionally centered instead on teaching Torah and deciding questions of Jewish law; by that definition, women can indeed be ordained as rabbis. These arguments are different in kind from changes adopted by liberal Judaism, often in disregard of Jewish law and tradition. There is a big difference between stretching a stocking and tearing it. It's designed to stretch.[11]

To the classical rabbis the restrictions that limited a woman's role in public worship were mere consequences, not ends in themselves. And they were minor consequences. Presiding, performing, and officiating have never meant much to Judaism. Far more important were rabbinic opinions that women should not be taught Talmud. But those opinions have been disregarded in the modern Orthodox community, embodying as they do only prejudice and no basic point of law.

Nowadays women are invited to study Talmud, or whatever they want.

Still, the nonexistence of female rabbis in normative Judaism has unquestionably taken on (for some women) the force of tragedy. Judaism can sympathize but can't do anything about it: if you create woman rabbis, you not only break the law, you break the poetry. And law and poetry are all there is.

I'll discuss the poetry of the situation later, but one aspect is simple. The roles of reader, singer, and officiator at synagogue were conceived for men in the same sense that the stage roles of Hamlet or Henry V were. A woman can say the words (as a man could play Rosalind or Lady Macbeth), but when it happens the result is unsatisfying and everyone knows it. One of the most thought-provoking moments I've experienced in synagogue recently came during remarks to the congregation by the daughter of an elderly man who had become a member. This synagogue was nominally "Conservative" but actually "Conservadox," which is part of the story: the prayers, readings, and tone of such (fairly uncommon) congregations are nearly Orthodox, except that men and women sit together.

Virtually all Conservative synagogues used to operate this way until the radical changes in Conservative Judaism of the early 1980s. No Conservative synagogue in years had reminded this elderly congregant of the synagogues he had known as a boy until he found this one. Here at last he felt at home.

He didn't know, or wouldn't tell, what made the difference, but the explanation is obvious: men were officiating, rather than men and women both. Co-ed Conservatism felt wrong to him. But no one had asked his opinion.

Who cares about an old man's preferences? Times change. But people don't go to synagogue to study social trends. They go to praise God and be close to their parents and grandparents, living and dead, and to the Jewish people as it has existed for countless generations. They bring their children to draw them close, too. Those who long to keep religion up to date miss the point. Religious practices do change, but must be moved as slowly and gently as a brimful glass of wine. Shimon bar Yohai tells us in a midrash not to change our ancestors' customs, and cites: "Remove not the ancient boundary stones, which thy fathers have set up" (Proverbs 22:28). Rabbi Yohanan agrees, and cites a different verse: "Heed the discipline of your father, and do not forsake the teaching of your mother" (Proverbs 1:8).

The woman who yearns to assume all the public roles of a contemporary rabbi resembles the foreign-born American citizen who wants to be president, or the man who yearns to be a hazzan but lacks the ear or voice for it, or hopes to be a *rosh yeshiva* (the head of a yeshiva is an honored leader of the community ex officio) but lacks the temperament or brains, or wants to be a poet but has nothing to say. In none of these cases can Judaism wave a wand and make the obstacles disappear. Opportunities and limitations are innate in who you are; accepting that fact is one of the stiffest trials of growing up. Almost every child who studies piano comes to realize at some point that he not going to be Rudolf Serkin. Nearly every physics student discovers that he is no Richard Feynman (let alone an Albert Einstein); most young tennis players dream of beating the pros but will never come close. Which does not mean that the way to be happy is to give up playing the piano or studying physics or playing tennis.

In the end, such issues have little to do with Judaism and much to do with character and personality. In *Persuasion* Jane Austen describes a woman who had once been rich, married, and happy but is now, though still young, a poor and ailing widow. She ought to be miserable but isn't. She has been given every reason but has declined them all. "Here was that elasticity of mind, that disposition to be comforted, that power of turning readily from evil to good, and of finding employment which carried her out of herself, which was from Nature alone. It was the choicest gift of heaven."[12]

And so we reach *erev Shabbat*, Friday evening—when the Sabbath begins; where the cult of the married couple settles down like a ruffled, beat-up, dead tired dove that has searched all week for a perch and has finally found one.

The Sabbath exists in two ways: as a weekly observance, the central shaping event of Jewish life, and as a sacred text to be read and pondered—a living poem that is enacted first, interpreted later.

To an observant Jewish family, the events and associations of Shabbat are well defined and concrete: the house is tidied and made ready, certain foods are prepared, special dinnerware and silverware usually appear—and onward through a list of particulars (families have their own preferences and traditions), of course including halakhic rules for Shabbat evening. These procedures bring great spiritual satisfaction. But following them doesn't necessarily mean that you think about them. Doesn't necessarily mean that you ponder their symbolic significance. Contemplation comes later. Which might explain why Jews are commanded in the Torah "to observe" and "to remember" the Sabbath—to act *and* (thoughtfully) recollect.

By the same token Wordsworth offers a famous definition of poetry: "emotion recollected in tranquility." No one in the grip of engrossing experience makes poetry at the same time. Afterward the poet mulls things over and thinks about the poetry he has lived through.

Why, then, does the woman of the house and not the man light and bless the candles on Friday night? I have already given a halakhic reason but there are other, poetic ones. (In other words, there are halakhic reasons and *Torat ha-lev* reasons.) One of Judaism's most important facets is also one of the hardest for outsiders to grasp: sacred persons and things are all colored "male" or "female," and the poetry of Judaism depends fundamentally on those colors. If you cannot see them, you mistake poetry for prose; you see a brightly colored world in black and white. If you refuse to see them, if you approach with a parochial unwillingness to grasp the basic difference between maleness and femaleness—to discriminate on the basis of sex—you will never see the spiritual aurora borealis that gives Judaism its uncanny glow.

The Sabbath is female, and Judaism proclaims its femaleness by having women create and embody it.

Why light candles? The Sabbath requires joy. Israel "must call the Sabbath joy," Isaiah proclaims (58:13). Light is necessary on Shabbat, Maimonides writes, because joy is necessary; to have joy, you need light. (It is strange and sad that Sabbatarians or Sabbath-observers among Puritan and other Protestant groups should have misused the biblical commandments to make their Sabbath Day dreary and joyless, a day of "perfect abstinence from any cheering employment.")[13]

Joy also suggests passion, and the possibility that Israel should greet the Sabbath as a groom greets his bride. On Friday evening at dusk, the Talmud reports, Rabbi Hanina would say, "Come let us go out to greet the bride, the queen. . . . Rabbi Yannai would robe himself, stand and say: Approach, bride!

Approach, bride!" Why did he do it? Out of religious duty, a
sense of obligation? No, Rashi explains; "out of love."

Joy is central to Shabbat—and is fundamental throughout the *Torat ha-lev*. George Orwell wrote, acutely, that a crucial problem of the modern age is "how to restore the religious
attitude while accepting death as final." Judaism does not accept death as final—although Jews are required to carry out
God's commandments for their own sakes, not in expectation
of a payoff in this life or the next. In any case, Orwell's problem
is no problem for Judaism; practicing Jews adopt the "religious
attitude" for the joy of it.

God's commandments bring joy. That they must be ob-
served joyfully is one of the most consistent themes of rabbinic
Judaism. And anyone who knows practicing Jews knows that
performing the commandments does indeed create joy.

One of the best-known passages in one of the best-
known volumes of the Talmud (Berakhot 31a) says that "we do
not stand to pray [that is, to say the *Amidah*, or Eighteen Bene-
dictions] in a state of sorrow, idleness, joking, bantering, light-
mindedness, or idle chatter, but in a state of joy in the commandment." (Of course, this is a deep and serious sort of joy.)
An echoing midrash tells us that "the Holy Spirit does not rest
where there is idleness, or sadness, or jesting, or joking, or
empty speech, but only where there is joy." This idea emerges
again and again; it is the topic of one of the most extraordinary
pronouncements in the Talmud: "What is the meaning of, 'For
the joy of the Lord is your strength' (Nehemiah 8:10)? . . . The
Holy One, blessed be He, said to Israel: My sons, borrow on my
account, and sanctify the day's sacredness, and trust Me; I will
repay" (Beitsah 15b).

The topic in this Talmudic passage is how to celebrate a
holiday properly. The rabbinic answer is to do it up right and

rejoice. "What gives me the right to rejoice?"—a question millions have asked themselves over the long, grim centuries. "What have I done to deserve it? And—do these times allow it?" But at the end of your life you won't regret having rejoiced, even when you did not deserve to; you will regret the times you could have rejoiced and didn't. So let God take this on Himself, says the Talmud: you be happy, while He settles the cosmic accounts. This "license to joy" cuts right to the heart of human nature.

Granted, a difficult commandment requiring self-sacrifice is much harder to carry out joyfully than the simple and beautiful requirements of ritual. But practicing Jews try to do every commandment joyfully, and some succeed. Some of Judaism's martyrs got joy from the very act of giving their lives for the sanctification of God's name. Such acts are beyond nearly all of us. But simple joy in the fulfillment of ordinary commandments is a driving force of Jewish life.

The woman of the house, who creates the Sabbath, symbolically embodies the Sabbath and the Sabbath bride. When she blesses the candles, Isaiah's voice echoes just out of hearing: "Arise, shine, for thy light is come!" (60:1). This verse is quoted in *L'kha dodi* ("Come, my darling"), the mystic hymn we sing to welcome the Sabbath bride every Friday evening. "Your God will rejoice over you," the hymn says, quoting Isaiah again (62:5), "as the bridegroom rejoices over the bride."

And why do we say that, with the Temple gone, the home has become Judaism's Holy of Holies? And women the ministering priesthood? The Sabbath is closely associated with the creation of the universe. It honors creation's completion. It celebrates the end of God's six days of creative labor. Now, the first thing God created was light; so it is fitting for more than one reason that the start of Shabbat be marked by the re-creation of light. ("Overdetermination" is typical of Judaism—the truth arriving like echoing river-sounds in a gorge, reaching you from many directions at once.)

The arrival of the holy Sabbath suggests also the arrival of God's presence, of the Shekhinah—who is female like a bride, and connected (like the Sabbath) to light. The Talmud calls the Shekhinah "radiant as the sun." *Kol kallah,* the voice of the bride, is the seductive voice of Shabbat.

Lit by the Shabbat flames she has just kindled, the woman's face recalls Moses' lit-up face when he climbs down from Sinai. Moses veiled his face (as I discussed in Chapter 3)—and when the woman screens her own lit-up face, the same theme-image unfolds. Why does she do it?—screen her face with her hands? Law and poetry are intertwined, closely embraced. In Judaism you pronounce a blessing and then do the act you have blessed. But this particular blessing creates Shabbat, and on Shabbat you may not light fires. So she lights the candles first, then covers her eyes and recites the blessing over the lights and only then, by uncovering her eyes (making herself like a bride when her veil is raised), she reveals the Shabbat lights to herself—as if she had brought them into being by her mere creative thought. The most spiritually powerful act in Judaism.

Thus the cult of the couple on Shabbat eve. The wife lights and blesses the candles, creating luminous joy and a symbol of the Shekhinah, re-creating the light of creation. Uncovering her eyes, she is symbolically transformed—she becomes the priestess in this Holy of Holies, the queenly Sabbath bride, the symbol of God's presence. The family sings a song of welcome to the ministering angels; they sing "Woman of Valor" to her, in praise of the Shekhinah, the Shabbat bride and

the housewife all at the same time. The husband blesses the wine
and they drink. He blesses two braided loaves and they eat.

Later, on Saturday night (as we saw in Chapter 2), they will
light a braided candle, bless more wine and fragrant spices—
and extinguish a multiwicked flame in the leftover wine.

And in the meantime? Why do Jews prepare for the Sabbath by reading the Song of Songs? What are a husband and
wife supposed to do on Friday night?

It takes no midrashic genius to notice that *erev Shabbat* is a
reenactment and confirmation of the wedding ceremony. The
same words—peace, joy, bride—predominate in both. And it
is hardly surprising that the Sabbath is associated with sex.
Perhaps the most decisive (and explicit) biblical comment on
marital sex is Proverbs 5:18–19:

> Get joy from the wife of your youth, lovely doe,
>     graceful gazelle; let her
> breasts satisfy you always; be staggered, always, by
>     her love.

These verses demand from a husband not merely fidelity but
devotion. They are an endorsement of sexual pleasure and passion; the purpose of sex is child-bearing *and* joy and comfort
and love. When David gets Batsheva pregnant and the infant
dies, husband and wife are heartbroken. "And David comforted
Batsheva; he came to her and slept with her" (2 Samuel 12:24).

So it is only natural that the Talmud should see Shabbat
as a sexual event. Isaiah commands, "call the Sabbath joy!"—
and the rabbis are not shy in spelling out exactly what that
command entails. Sexual relations, the Talmud says, are espe-

cially blessed on the Sabbath, and Torah scholars in particular are required to make love to their wives on Friday night. In his hymn for Sabbath evening, the sixteenth century mystic Isaac Luria spells it out: "He gives her joy / in twofold measure. / Lights shining / and streams of blessing."

Israel's worship is wholly and deliberately divorced from pagan imagery and ritual. Virile, violent, lustful, blazing-phallus gods and whoring goddesses, stacked and fertile—the Bible turns away in disgust. But Scripture does discuss the covenant between God and Israel in terms of marriage; and in this marriage Israel is the (often misbehaving) bride. "For your maker is your husband. . . . Can one reject the wife of his youth?" (Isaiah 54:5,6—and other related phrases elsewhere, as I have mentioned). For the rabbis, the Song of Songs itself sets out the relationship between God and Israel in a way that remains startling: God as male suitor, Israel as the (active) female object of God's desire. Marriage is no concession to human needs, no pragmatic arrangement; it is the culminating step in the creation of man, and it is a hint (distant and rough and provisional, but a hint) of what exists between man and God.

The rabbis take the hint. They also run it in reverse. In Deuteronomy the Torah is described as Israel's inheritance; to make an interpretative point, they re-read the word "inheritance," *morashah*, as *me'urasah*, betrothed, wife-to-be; thus the Torah becomes female and Israel (in relationship) male.

Not that man-and-Torah-scroll is a sublimated version of man-and-wife. The intention is to describe the connection between Jews and the Torah as so vivid and passionate, it recalls the connection between man and woman. Like man and wife, Israel and the Torah are one. Unity is the real theme of this chapter, Judaism's version of nuclear fusion: the creation of one out of two—with the huge birth of energy that accompanies such unifications. (Consult any physics text.)

And so we return to Rabbi Akiba and his wife Rachel. She is a celebrated figure in the Talmud.

The rabbis ask, "Who is rich?" Rabbi Akiba's answer: "He who has a wife whose deeds are beautiful." Which is merely interesting until we realize that Akiba is not making an abstract pronouncement or launching an edifying platitude or talking feminism. He is speaking about his own wife.

She had insisted that, although he was an adult with his own household, he was ignorant of Torah and should therefore drop everything and go get educated. And she waited faithfully while he did. He departed for years of study, then went away again and studied some more, until he had become the leading sage of his generation. Whereupon, surrounded by his disciples, he announced that he owed everything and they owed everything to her. He became great because she was already great.

In answering "Who is rich?" Akiba turned his own upwelling love into a universal principle and put it at the center of rabbinic Judaism. We visit this ever-flowing spring at Judaism's center the way people once visited the well at the center of town, again and again. More than anyone else, Akiba built the Bible's predisposition into Judaism's cult of marriage, based on an acute awareness of the perfect asymmetry of creation. The miracle of human creation, when male and female come together to make a man, hints at the eventual miracle of salvation—when God and mankind come together to make the realm of the messiah and the world to come.

When he made his startling statement about the Song of Songs, Akiba changed Judaism forever. Playing on its name, he said that the Song of Songs is no less than the Holy of Holies; furthermore, that if you weigh the whole world against the day Israel received the Song of Songs . . . the day of the Song wins. Its value is greater. It is worth more. The Song is monumentally holy. It outweighs, in some sense, the whole rest of the universe put together.

Why did he say it? Why did this inspired and beloved teacher, humane thinker, dedicated patriot, and holy martyr teach that, when you visit the innermost precincts of Judaism, you arrive at the unrestrained, almost unseemly joy of the Song of Songs? Looking at the austere gray walls of Judaism from outside, who would have guessed it?

When Newton grasped the idea of universal gravitation, it was the greatest achievement in the history of science. Some say the vision was triggered by a falling apple. Maybe not, but the details don't matter. The apple is plausible: one day, Newton understood the whole physical structure of the universe; it all came clear to him when (perhaps) he saw an apple fall. Akiba did something even greater: one day he understood the whole moral structure of the universe. "This is Akiba's midrash," writes Judah Goldin in a magnificent essay.[14] "Before all the world Israel is to proclaim what *love* of God is." And why did Akiba say it? Because he loved his wife. It all came clear to him when (perhaps) he held his wife in his arms.

In the next chapter we will see how the creation of the people Israel was incomplete—and how it was up to the Jews, each Jew one-by-one, to finish the work. The same holds for the universe itself. It is commanded that every Jew must write a whole Torah scroll by himself. But few can do it, and in practice the law is lenient. The scribe leaves a few letters carefully outlined but empty; when you ink them in, you are said to have performed the commandment and written the scroll. The

*Torat ha-lev* suggests that God did (in effect) the same thing when He created the universe. He left an unfinished letter as an invitation to each married couple to finish the work of creation.

Perhaps there is one letter that is filled in again and again. Perhaps there are many. But when a man and a woman marry, the universe pauses (maybe the angels hold their breath?)—waiting to see whether the couple have it in them to finish the work of creation. "For man is not so called except when male and female are one."

To sum up, here again are the questions:

> Isn't normative or Orthodox Judaism inherently anti-woman, insofar as its public ceremonies are conducted by males? Assuming we reject the idea that women are in any way inferior, aren't we forced to make basic changes in Judaism?
>
> In more positive terms: how does Judaism understand sexuality, the family, and relationships between man and woman?

No one can deny that the Bible and the rabbinic classics emerged from a world in which men dominated women physically, legally, and economically. No one can deny of Orthodox Judaism that its public face in synagogue is male. And those who believe that equal treatment for women demands that men and women be interchangeable will find that Orthodox Judaism falls short in many other ways, too.

Yet those who prefer tolerance to intolerance will find it easy to acquit normative Judaism of anti-woman bias. The role women play in Judaism's daily life is too central and too charged with religious and poetic meaning to allow such a charge to stick. A religious system that has survived and kept the Jewish family together for millennia deserves at the very least to be judged fairly before we rush to alter its most basic arrangements.

The family is Judaism's central reality. Shabbat is a celebration of the married couple; it is also, as such, a celebration of sexuality and of sexual union. For Judaism a man in full requires male and female components. A male or female alone is only half a man.

But "half" means that the two pieces are equal in importance, not interchangeable. Two perfectly asymmetric halves are like the black type and surrounding whiteness on this page, like the man's lips and the woman's when they kiss, like the grape's pulp and its skin. Perfect, interchangeable symmetry is ordinary next to the mystery and beauty of man and woman's perfect asymmetry.

# V

# Inward Pilgrimage

Finally we reach the hardest, deepest problem any religious believer faces: the question of evil. How can we accept the simultaneous existence of a just, all-powerful God and a merciless world? When innocent human beings are hurt or destroyed by cruelty and violence we *must* ask, with Macduff, "Did heaven look on and would not take their part?" We must entertain the grim hypothesis associated in some sources with the second century heretic Elishah ben Abuya: *Leit din ve-leit dayan,* "there is no judgment and no judge."

Investigating this problem requires, to start, that we consider the underlying theme of the Five Books of Moses as we did in the case of halakha. The Pentateuch (or Torah proper) has a clear narrative direction from Creation and the epochal emergence of Abraham through the growth, enslavement, and liberation of the Jewish nation and its arrival at the brink of the Promised Land. Many separate, varied stories make up this narrative, and much legal material is mixed in. But taken as a whole, does the Pentateuch have a theme, aside from the forward motion of the narrative and the unfolding of divine law in its pre-rabbinic form? The answer is yes, there is a theme—one that tells us something basic not only about the Torah but about Judaism's view of God and history. The same theme also suggests Judaism's answer to the question of evil.

Judaism's way is a path of joy and life—but is no easy road to follow. As we consider this hardest of all questions, we reach the roughest parts of the path—and ideas that some readers may be unwilling or unable to accept. Which is not surprising; after all, this last of our multilayered theme-images begins with the hardest journey any man ever made. "Long is the way / and hard that out of Hell leads up to light" (Milton's *Paradise Lost* 2:432–433).

What does the veil image of Chapter 3 yield? You can sense God's reality and be inspired or "in-spirited" by His presence just beyond the veil. Your own spirit expands when your mind draws in the boundless idea of God as your chest did once when you pulled in the deepest of all conceivable breaths on the brightest, most boundless morning of your life.

The veil image shows us, too, how Judaism has repeatedly shattered singular objects or events—Moses' career, the Holy of Holies, the burning bush—into prismatic fragments whose crystalline glitter overlays the whole space and time of Jewish history. A shattered-scattered figure, object, event is re-created (reemerges) out of its countless far-flung fragments—as an eminent teacher lives on in the sum of his disciples.[1] When a beloved person dies, those who most loved him or her are driven (unawares) to become him as best they can, each in his own way. Any much-loved person's life on earth is extended and diffused by these faithful mourners and eventually dissolves into the ocean of his people.

God Himself remains beyond the veil, outside the universe in His own realm that seems to include yet to be utterly separate from ours. But Jews insist on confronting God. How can they?

In Chapter 3 we considered an indirect way to do it: by means of the veil itself. Now, another way—a direct way—and a fourth theme of the *Torat ha-lev:* inward pilgrimage. The theme is associated with a striking characteristic of some of the Bible's most important stories: the coincidence of (so to speak) epiphany and theophany; of a man's comprehending his own character at the same time he encounters the Lord. Jews find God beyond the universe *and* in a still, small voice that comes from deep inside. When they confront that inner voice and do what it says, they become part of the most important "re-creation" of all: they put God on earth. They allow His actual presence to reemerge.

Like perfect asymmetry, the inward pilgrimage is an unfamiliar image. In some ways it is the veil's opposite; in others, the two are a matched set, spiritual bookends. The veil has to do with stretching outward, this new theme with reaching inward. Both routes lead to the same place.

Abraham is the founder of Judaism. His story rests on two identical commands direct from God. This repeated command is *lekh l'kha,* meaning "move yourself," "get thee out," "pick yourself up," "get going." It first occurs when God tells Abraham, "Move yourself from your land, from your birthplace, from your father's house, to the land that I will show you" (Genesis 12:1). It appears again at the beginning of the Akedah, the famous story of the binding of Isaac. God "tests" Abraham by telling him, take your son Isaac and move yourself to the land of Moriah and offer him there as a sacrifice (Genesis 22:2).

It is an axiom of rabbinic commentary that the Torah wastes no words.[2] In the phrase "move yourself," what does "yourself" (*l'kha*) tell us? Why not just plain "move!"?

Commenting on the first appearance of this phrase in Genesis 12:1, the Zohar offers an opinion: "yourself" is a clue that God actually intends an inner journey. He means to tell Abraham, "Move *into* yourself." (Literally, *l'kha* means "to you," and the Zohar translates the reflexive command *lekh l'kha* not as "you—go!" but as "go to you," meaning "go to yourself" or "go *into* yourself.") Once again rabbinic interpretation has used an ancient rule of reading to expose a rushing undercurrent of meaning.

What does the undercurrent tell us?

We start by noticing the climax of the Akedah, where an angel calls to Abraham "from the heavens" and orders him not to sacrifice his son. This heavenly voice conveys an authentic divine message, and must be obeyed.

Yet ordinarily the Talmud takes a very different view of heavenly voices. It tells us to ignore them. "We pay no attention to a *bat kol*" (Baba Metzia 59b): literally, to a "daughter of a voice"—a beautiful way to say "echo" or refer to any voice that seems to speak God's words but is not accompanied by the overwhelming, unmistakable experience of direct revelation. You might think that a voice from heaven (if you are lucky enough to hear one) means that you have hit the spiritual jackpot. But the Talmud says, ignore it!

The passage in Baba Metzia goes even further. In a celebrated proclamation, Rabbi Yehoshua invokes a phrase in Deuteronomy—"it is not in the heavens" (32:12)—to announce that the Torah itself, since it is no longer on high but is right here on earth, is *man's* to interpret: man and not God has the final say on the laws of Judaism; man and not God has become (by God's own design) the final authority.[3] So don't go craning your necks, scanning the skies, or watching the cosmic news-wire for meaningful portents. Do not seek, expect, or even pay attention to divine or seemingly divine pronouncements from nature or beyond nature. Religious truth is not in the heavens, it is right here on earth.

But exactly where? And how do we find it?

Many generations after the great communal revelation of the Ten Commandments, the prophet Elijah returns to the mountain called Horeb—another name for Sinai. He is told to stand there before the Lord. He watches and waits. A great wind comes up; but "the Lord was not in the wind." Then an earthquake—but "the Lord was not in the earthquake." Then a fire, but "the Lord was not in the fire." And after the fire, "a still, small voice." Where once God's voice was powerful and terrifying, now at the very same spot it has grown still and small.

This small voice must be different from those heavenly voices the Talmud wants us to ignore. But just what is it?

And while we are asking, here is another question from a different and seemingly unrelated realm. What does it mean that the main façade of nearly every synagogue in the world is not the external façade facing the street but the "internal" façade leading to the ark? In part this architectural fact speaks merely of the Jewish desire to keep a low profile; is a response to Gentile hostility. But there is more to it.

Even in such medieval synagogues as the Altneuschul in Prague or the reconstructed synagogue of Worms, where the ark is relatively plain and small, the building's main façade is still its interior façade—which is framed with emphatic dignity no matter how old or plain the synagogue, and which offers a door or entranceway at the top of its own flight of steps. The stairs and frame grow larger and fancier as the centuries pass. Often the ark has several doors side by side, like the ceremonial entrance to a public building. And even in synagogues where the ark is freestanding, it takes on the character of a grand entrance.

Why? What does this mean?

Once Jews made pilgrimages to Jerusalem, where the high priest entered the Holy of Holies on the Temple Mount. The architecture of the synagogue offers a commentary on those long-ago spiritual journeys. You are inside already, but when you throw open the doors of the ark you prepare to go further inside. You are about to enter . . . what?

Now we are ready for that fourth principal element of the *Torat ha-lev*. We are ready for the "move!" that implies no physical motion, the grand entryway you cannot (bodily) enter; for the still, small voice that can only be an *inner* voice; for the inward pilgrimage to find yourself and your God. "For the Lord searches all hearts, and understands all the mind's inclinations; if you seek Him, He will be found by you" (I Chronicles 28:9).

Some ceremonies can be interpreted as sacred drama—as moving, speaking images. For example: go through the gate into the women's court at the Second Temple, up the stairs of lapped semicircles and through another gate to the court of the Israelites, into the court of priests, onto the porch, into the sanctuary, past one curtain, past another, and there before you: the Holy of Holies. Or: push aside the ark curtain in synagogue, open the doors, remove the Torah, carry it to the reading stand, remove the breastplate, the crown or the *rimmonim*, and the silver pointer; then the mantle; then untie the wrapper and (finally) roll open the scroll—and there before you: the words themselves.

That is one image of inward pilgrimage. Nietzsche shows us a different image. He speaks of "anyone who has sat alone with his soul in intimate dispute and dialogue, year in and year out, day and night, anyone who has become a cave bear or treasure hunter or treasure guard and dragon in his cave (which might be a labyrinth but also a gold mine)." With his biblical education and spiritual intuition, Nietzsche sometimes describes Jewish reality without knowing it.

In the *Torat ha-lev*, finding God and finding your own self are two aspects of one problem: at the destination of your inward pilgrimage you are confronted by Him *and* you. "And God said, let us make man in our image, after our likeness" (Genesis 1:26). If the image (when you find Him) looks somehow like you, don't be surprised. That is how you were made: in God's image. When you reach God's glory you see yourself from God's vantage point—as if you were standing outside the universe looking in.

If separation is the great theme of halakha, inward pilgrimage is the theme of biblical narrative, and biblical heroes embark repeatedly on journeys that turn out to be inward pilgrimages. The physical journey alerts us to an underlying spiritual one.

The central, most characteristic inward pilgrimage in the Bible is Israel's from slavery in Egypt to freedom and nationhood in the promised land. Clearly this is a journey to self-knowledge. A disorganized slave-people—perfectly suited to the "slave morality" that Nietzsche despises (and wrongly associates with Judeo-Christianity in general)—is led to see itself as God's chosen nation, recipient of God's Torah, designated occupant of God's holy land; practitioner by divine command of a morality holier and nobler than anything Nietzsche ever described.

Equally (or nearly as) important is the inward pilgrimage of Moses—from his aristocratic childhood among Egyptian nobles, set apart from God and his tortured people, to his climb up Mount N'vo at the very end, to a place where the promised land lies at his feet and he knows that he will never reach it. Moses' journey takes him upward from self-ignorance and turmoil to self-knowledge and peace as God's foremost prophet and (perhaps) God's only "friend" in all the universe.

Moses' pilgrimage shows all mankind what life is. The proof is in the upward struggle.

But even before Moses, each of the patriarchs, and Jacob's son Joseph, makes his own inward pilgrimage. Abraham was the first, starting from paganism and his homeland and arriving at Judaism and the land of Israel. (I've referred to Moses as God's "friend," but here is Coleridge: "If ever man could, without impropriety, be called, or supposed to be, 'the friend of God,' Abraham was that man.") Isaac makes an inward pilgrimage of sorts when he accompanies Abraham in the Akedah, which I discuss below. Jacob escapes to his uncle Laban and returns to face his brother Esau. Joseph's journey takes him from pampered, brilliant, obnoxious childhood to his appointment as the second most powerful man in Egypt— who has nonetheless learned humility, and how to forgive. The Bible's sense of irony and moral grandeur are never more plain than in this famous story of the impotent, arrogant child who becomes an all-powerful, compassionate man.

The Akedah ranks among the small handful of mankind's most intensely studied stories. We know the plot, and tend to take the details for granted. But if we listen as if for the first time, we can hear its strangeness.

At God's command, Abraham and his son Isaac walk

three days and arrive at Moriah at last. But why does Abraham
have to "move himself" at all? What purpose does the three-
day journey serve? God might have fixed the sacrifice of Isaac
for right now, on the spot—and found out just as surely
whether Abraham had it in him to offer up his beloved son.[4]

The Ramban quotes Rabbi Akiba saying, in a midrash,
that the three days' walk was intended to show the world that
Abraham was acting deliberately and not "in confusion," as if
stunned or overwhelmed by the divine command. This sounds
like the right answer to the wrong question. The Ramban
seems in reality to be explaining why God tells Abraham "*kakh
na*," using a gentle imperative—"would you take your son?"—
instead of just "take him!" God does it to make plain that He
has no intention of overawing or overwhelming Abraham. He
speaks as if to a friend. And the steady, even tone in which
Abraham's preparations are described next morning shows
that Abraham is indeed not flustered, not overwhelmed.

But again: why the three-day trip? It is an important
question, because this detail is one of the most shocking in the
whole Bible. If "sacrifice your son" is immeasurably cruel,
"sacrifice your son three days from now"—after three days of
torturing anticipation—is immeasurably crueler. Unless this
detail shocks us right down to our feet, we are not reading the
story at all. Common sense—never mind philosophy or theology—forces us to conclude that the three-day journey must
somehow change the nature of the test itself. It can't be a mere
narrative quirk. It must serve a purpose. (In *Genesis: The Beginning of Desire* [1995], Avivah Gottlieb Zornberg notes the
Talmudic view that, in some cases, a long trip made on purpose to perform a commandment increases the ultimate value
of the deed when it is done. This might be part of the explana-

tion we seek, but could hardly be the whole reason for Abraham's horrible journey.)

And the trip does serve an essential purpose—if we understand "move yourself" as the Zohar understands it. The Zohar's reading of *lekh l'kha* offers a radical re-understanding of Abraham's test. Perhaps the test was not to *act*, not to "offer up your son"; such an act requires (after all) a moment's willpower or delirium—and once it is done, it is done forever. But maybe the test was to *believe*. Recall that Abraham "believed in the Lord, who accounted it to him for righteousness" (Genesis 15:6).

Of course, anyone might believe anything for a moment; to believe for a moment proves nothing. An act that takes a moment might change the world, but a momentary belief is meaningless in itself. And here is where "three days" come in. Abraham's trial was to *sustain* his belief over three long days—the three longest of his life. Did Abraham truly "believe in the Lord"? Without those three days, the test is meaningless; with them, it is one of the hardest trials a man could endure. God's question was not, "will you sacrifice your son?" Instead it was: "will you have faith in Me and My covenant and believe that I will *not let* you sacrifice your son?" Will Abraham believe this and go on believing it, hour by hour, mile by mile, step by step? Will he go on believing, as time grows short, that God will intervene before it is too late?

This is not the traditional way to read the story. But every word of the story is consistent with the conventional reading *and* this unconventional one. To know for sure which is right, we would have to know Abraham's mind: is he thinking, "I am going to sacrifice my son," or "I am *not* going to"? But as the literary philosopher Erich Auerbach notes in the famous first chapter of *Mimesis*, the Bible is careful to give us no shred of a direct report on Abraham's mental state.

So we are left with this. In one of literature's most celebrated exchanges, Isaac says to his father: "Here are the fire and the wood, but where is the lamb for the burnt-offering?" Abraham answers, "God will provide Himself with the lamb for a burnt-offering, my son" (Genesis 22:7–8). When he "uttered those words," Shalom Spiegel writes in *The Last Trial*, his definitive study of the Akedah literature, Abraham's "only purpose at the time was to put Isaac off." That is the universal consensus. But there is a simpler explanation: when he said, "God will provide Himself with the lamb for a burnt-offering," Abraham was telling the truth just as he saw it.

He had spent three long days traveling into himself—fulfilling the command "move into yourself," as the Zohar has it. He had spent three long days testing his belief in God and God's covenant. Was it solid enough to walk on? Would it bear his weight and his son's? He had emerged knowing the reality of his faith—faith not in the sense of blind obedience; faith in God's goodness and truth. Abraham emerges from the trial, Kierkegaard writes, with his faith solidified; "after passing through the dark gate the believing man steps forth into the everyday which is henceforth hallowed as the place in which he has to live with mystery" (*Fear and Trembling*, 1843). Abraham's walk to Moriah was an inward pilgrimage. He emerged from his long, hard trial knowing God and himself.

Note again how well this reading fits the Bible's view of Abraham, whose faith in God is singled out for praise in the verse (Genesis 15:6) I quoted above, one that is highly significant to Jews (and to Christians also).[5] Abraham is praised not for obedience but for belief. Had obedience been all-important, a test of obedience might have been called for—

and the Akedah is usually read just that way, as a test of obedience. But since Abraham's belief in God (which suggests trust in God, belief in God's righteousness) and *not* merely his obedience was singled out, a test of belief fits perfectly into the narrative—and becomes a plausible way to read the Akedah.

Leon Kass, one of the sharpest of modern commentators, considers but dismisses the idea that Abraham understands his trial as a test of faith; dismisses the idea that Abraham tells himself, in Kass's words, that "God doesn't really mean it." He rejects this interpretation because, if it were true, "the story makes no sense as a test and loses all its horror." If Abraham believes all along that Isaac will survive, where is the challenge? Where is the trial?

But Kass has not (it seems to me) accounted sufficiently for those three long days. To believe that God will step in and save you, and to have your belief confirmed on the spot, would indeed be no test. To believe that God will step in and save you and to *sustain* that belief for a whole day and another and the start of a third; to pit your faith against the growing anxiety that clutches tighter with every step, that dries your throat and makes your hands damp and fingers cold and your pulse beat in your ears as you swallow anguish (suppose I am wrong?) and walk on, step by step by step, and build an altar, and arrange the wood, and bind your son, and lay him on the altar, and reach out your hand, and take the heavy knife, and raise it high, and hold your breath—

Is it true that this story "makes no sense as a test and loses all its horror"?

A subjective question. Each reader must decide for himself.

The Akedah is unique. But in the largest sense it is Israel's story, struggling toward Moriah through history, step by step, with everything at stake and nothing but faith and a promise to go on. The inward pilgrimage is fundamental to the Bible and to all Judaism.

God is (among other things) a mirror that gives man back to himself—after disentangling his soul from everything irrelevant and superficial. Early Hasidic thinkers taught that *heshbon ha-nefesh,* self-scrutiny, was an essential part of prayer. Maimonides was acutely aware that to be a Jew requires that you know yourself; to know God *is* to know yourself. He writes in the first book of the *Mishneh Torah* that "our ancient sages exhorted us that a person should always evaluate his dispositions." He writes similar things in his commentary on the Mishnah tractate Avot (often called "Ethics of the Fathers" in English, *Perek,* for short, in Hebrew). The eminent scholar Isadore Twersky tells us that Maimonides saw Avot as "a special treatise on the therapy of the soul," and believed that "one who hopes to regulate the soul must be acquainted with the faculties of the soul, just as the physician must know the parts of the body."

Maimonides, writes the commentator Almut Bruckstein, "seems to suggest that the ultimate task of knowing God and walking in His ways is inextricably linked to a critical assessment of one's own character."

God gives man back to himself: true for the individual and for mankind at large. The Bible's stories of inward pilgrimage show God doing just this, in narratives of remarkable depth and psychological penetration.

Suppose Moses had looked in a mirror that showed him the psychic, spiritual truth about himself. Hamlet says to his mother: "You go not till I have set you up a glass / Where you may see the inmost part of you." What would Moses have seen in Hamlet's glass? In a mirror that showed a man's spirit, not merely his outside?

Moses is a fiery, passionate man who burns with a sense of mission. In the very first deed reported of him in the Bible, he kills with one powerful stroke an Egyptian who is beating a Hebrew. But someone saw him do it, and he is forced to run for his life. All alone with Jethro's flock in the wilds of Midian, "beyond the wilderness," what thoughts would Moses be turning over? "I have seen yes *seen* the affliction of my people in Egypt, and I have heard their screams in the face of their taskmasters; I do know their sufferings" (Exodus 3:7).

Seething at Egyptian oppression, capable of great passionate deeds: it fits perfectly that Moses should take it on himself to lead his people to freedom. Naturally he would agonize over his ability to carry the thing off—"The man Moses was very humble, more so than any man on the face of the earth" (Numbers 12:3). Yet, being the man he was, how could he not have screwed his courage to the sticking place and set off? "I have seen yes *seen* the affliction of my people in Egypt"—the voice is the voice of Moses, but the Lord is speaking. At the bush Moses hears what is on his own mind; he listens (as it were) to his own soul speaking.

And how would the "inmost part" of Moses have appeared in Hamlet's glass? Like a "bush burning with fire; yet the bush is not consumed" (Exodus 3:2): that would be perfect. A midrash speaks of this thornbush ("thornbush" is the literal meaning of the word usually translated "bush") as the humblest of trees—a fit symbol for Moses, the humblest of men. That the bush is on fire but not consumed makes it a perfect picture of the man Moses—passionate, humble, and supremely tough; a man who burns with a sense of duty; a man who is capable—although he strenuously resists admitting it—of confronting Pharaoh and leading the fractious and difficult Israelites through the wilderness to the land of Israel. Moses is capable, in other words, of undertaking a mission that would have consumed a lesser man, as flames would have consumed an ordinary bush. The burning bush is a character sketch of Moses in the form of an image.

At the bush, Moses hears his own mind speaking *and* looks at (or into) his inner self. But instead of telling us about this psychological event, the story *shows* us Moses confronting a physical embodiment of his character and psyche. And of course this physical embodiment of Moses' inner self is, at the same time, the scene of divine revelation. This epiphany is also a theophany—as if God's presence creates a brilliant flash that lights up man's psyche to the core. ("The words of Torah," says a midrash, "are like golden vessels: the more you scour and polish them, the more they shine and reflect the face of he who looks at them.") Kierkegaard comments on (in effect) theophany as epiphany in a profound yet simple analogy. "A cattleman who (if this were possible) is a self directly before his cattle is a very low self." Our sense of self changes when someone is watching—depending on who the someone is. (When surgeons in French North Africa were forced to operate on wounded soldiers without anesthetics during the Second World War, their patients were better able to bear pain when female nurses were looking on.)[6] Kierkegaard continues: "What infinite reality the self gains by being conscious of existing before God! ... In fact, the greater the conception of God, the more self there is; the more self, the greater the conception of God" (*Sickness unto Death*, 1849).

The truths about himself revealed to Moses at the burning bush are not easy truths for a man to confront. Egypt draws him irresistibly, but Egypt is dangerous ground; Pharaoh himself wants Moses dead (Exodus 2:13). That the bush is on fire but not consumed reminds us that Moses will die in old age with "his eyes undimmed and his powers unabated." But the image seems to warn him, also, that he will burn with passion his whole life and never be done burning; never cool down, cool off, come to rest. And he dies without setting foot in the land of Israel; with his passion, in this sense, unconsummated. Moses would have been subliminally aware of these truths, or something like them; but at the burning bush they cry out to him and he must listen and accept his destiny, as he learns it from God and his own soul. The encounter at the bush is a theological *and* psychological event.

God has become Hamlet's glass—or Hamlet's glass has become God's veil. By journeying to the other side of the wilderness and coming at last upon the Lord, Moses has pushed into himself farther and farther and discovered—or owned up to—the truth of his own nature. At the burning bush, God reveals Moses to himself.

One last element of this story. Moses reaches his epochal encounter with God not in but "beyond" the desert—on the desert's far side. ("He led the flock to the backside of the desert, and came to the mountain of God" [Exodus 3:1].) There is nothing easy or routine about finding God. (The eminent historian and Catholic theologian Michael Novak ponders this fact in his powerful *No One Sees God: The Dark Night of Atheists and Believers,* 2008.) The story of the burning bush shows us that Moses had to push through the wilderness from one side to the other to encounter the Lord; *after* the wilderness came God. In the Puritan allegory *Pilgrim's Progress* (by John Bunyan, 1684), the hero must pass through Vanity Fair to reach the Celestial City; in our more introspective text, Moses must

pass through a lonely wasteland to reach God and himself. Of
course, the book of Exodus is not (unlike *Pilgrim's Progress*)
explicit allegory. Were we meant to read "beyond the wilderness" this way, or does it merely lend itself to this reading? We
don't know. But "any great artist is symbolic without knowing
it," wrote G. K. Chesterton.[7] Among other things, the Bible is
certainly great art. It is also deeper and more subtle than any
explicit allegory. "A symbol always transcends the one who
makes use of it," wrote Albert Camus, "and makes him say in
reality more than he is aware of expressing."[8]

Can an image capture deep psychological truth? Modern
intellectual life likes to ignore such questions. Yet the Bible and
the *Torat ha-lev* revolve around just this sort of psychologically
revealing image. Each one of us (for that matter) confronts this
sort of image all the time—in our dreams.

One of the most dramatic examples of the Lord veiled
behind Hamlet's glass occurs in three short verses in Exodus—
the strangest story in the Bible. I have analyzed this passage
(Exodus 4:26–28) in my book *The Muse in the Machine* (1994).
Here I will focus on one part of it: the part that makes Moses'
confrontation with God seem like a confrontation with his
own self.

The incident takes place on the road from Midian back to
Egypt. Moses was born in Egypt, but had gone away and married a Midianite woman named Tsipporah. His daily routine
was shattered when he met God at the burning bush and was
ordered back to Egypt to free his fellow Israelites. He sets out,
but on the way, "It happened on the road, at an overnight stopping place, that the Lord met him and tried to kill him. But
Tsipporah took a flint, cut off her son's foreskin and touched it
to his feet; she said 'You are my bloodied bridegroom!' And he
withdrew from him. That was when she said 'bloodied bride-

groom' with respect to the circumcision." ("His feet" might be a euphemism for "his genitals.")

The questions are gross and obvious. This is a story (one feels) that no one has understood for thousands of years. Why should the Lord try to kill Moses? How does Tsipporah know how to respond? How should we understand the phrase "bloodied bridegroom" (or, in the usual translation, "bloody bridegroom")?

In his Genesis commentary, the distinguished German scholar Gerhard von Rad summarizes his own view in a single offhand sentence: "The extremely old story in Exodus 4:24 ff. cannot properly be understood at all." So much for higher criticism. The idea of inward pilgrimage offers a more fruitful way of reading.

Start with the unsettling violence of our story. Moses faces a staggering surprise attack. He is saved by the slash of a knife. Blood flows, his wife streaks him with the blood and then pronounces the story's weird central phrase. The Hebrew *damim* (plural of *dam*, "blood") refers most often to blood violently spilt.

This undertone of violence will help us see the story for what it is.

Moses is on his way home to Egypt. An initial clue emerges when we remember why he left Egypt in the first place: he had run for his life. He had come upon an Egyptian beating a Hebrew and, seeing no bystanders, had struck the Egyptian down—had killed him and hidden the body in a shallow sandy grave (Exodus 2:11–14). This was no casual act: you have to hit a man hard to kill him with a stick. But Moses hadn't looked round carefully enough, or else the Hebrew he saved betrayed him—because the act became public knowledge. When Pharaoh found out, "he sought to kill Moses" (Exodus

2:15). How do we understand Moses in this story? "One can only get on his track, indeed," wrote Franz Kafka in another context, "when one gives oneself up to his train of thought, painful as it may be."[9]

Ordering Moses back to Egypt, God had reassured him that "all the men who sought your life are dead" (Exodus 4:19). But has the affair of the murdered Egyptian really been laid to rest? Or has it merely been hastily covered over, like the dead Egyptian? Note that Moses did not bury the body. He only hid it, "in the sand" (2:12).

In fact, *concealment* is a central theme of Moses' life. In his infancy he is concealed by his mother in riverside rushes. Later he kills an Egyptian and hides the body—and when it is discovered, catastrophe follows. "So this thing is known!" he says to himself in fear. When he flees to Midian, the way in which Reuel's daughters describe him to their father is notable: "An Egyptian," they report, "saved us from the shepherds" (2:19). Naturally! Moses had been reared in Pharaoh's court; he could hardly *not* have been Egyptian in dress and speech and habits and manners.

Did he ever correct his future in-laws' misimpression? The question would be out of bounds and irrelevant if concealment were not so important to his story. But listen to him explaining to his father-in-law the sudden decision to return to Egypt: "Let me go and return to my brothers who are in Egypt, and see if they are still alive" (4:18). A strange, awkward speech. Moses evidently does not add that his "brothers in Egypt" do not happen to be Egyptian. Do his wife and family know he is an Israelite? Again the question would be inappropriate and irrelevant—except that the story of the bloodied bridegroom seems to revolve around an infant circumcision that did *not* take place. Evidently Moses' own son has not been circumcised.

Circumcision was widespread in the Middle East, but seems ordinarily to have been performed during childhood or at puberty. (Among the Egyptians in particular, circumcision is supposed by modern scholars to have been a puberty rite.)

Israelite circumcision was different. It took place on the eighth day after birth. This is a crucial obligation in the Bible and in all of Judaism. (In a midrash, Tsipporah is said to have exclaimed: "How great is the power of circumcision. Here my husband deserved death for having shirked this mitzvah!")

Suppose that, on reaching Midian, Moses was introduced to his future in-laws as an Egyptian; suppose he reveals exactly nothing about his mission on departing. Shortly after his departure, the Lord attacks him—and the attack seems to hinge on the *omission* of a ritual that marks out a family as Israelite. Is the story hinting (or implicitly assuming) that Moses—who was hidden in the rushes, who hid his victim's body in the sand—leaves Midian with his identity still hidden?

Let's leave that question aside for a moment. The medieval commentator Abraham ibn Ezra directs our attention to the story's broader context. The phrase "she touched his feet" in verse 25 is ambiguous; does "his feet" mean Moses' feet or his son's? The reference is to Moses, writes ibn Ezra, "as in 'When He sees the blood on the lintel He will not permit the destroyer'" to enter. The citation is Exodus 12:23, the night of the first Passover. On that night, as on the night of our story, the threatened are protected by a sign of blood.

What is this blood sign, and what does it mean? If concealment is a basic theme for Moses, firstborns are basic to the larger story of Passover and Exodus. God's challenge to Pharaoh could not possibly have been more direct: "Thus says the Lord: Israel is my first-born son. I have said to you, send forth my son so that he may serve me; but you have refused to send him forth. Behold: I will kill *your* first-born son" (Exodus 4: 22–23). On the night of the first Passover, Egypt's firstborn die but Israel's survive—because Israelite homes are marked by the blood of the Passover lamb smeared on their doorposts. This blood sign distinguishes the Lord's firstborn from Pharaoh's.

So Israel collectively is the Lord's firstborn. A privileged position—with a catch. Firstborns are forfeit to the Lord. "Every opener of a womb among the children of Israel, whether man or beast, is mine" (Exodus 13:2). (The Torah ties this obligation specifically to the night of the Passover.) When are firstborns forfeit? "On the eighth day you will give it to me" (Exodus 22:29).

Firstborn animals are sacrificed; firstborn sons are (of course) not sacrificed but "redeemed," in a ceremony that is also described in the Bible. The symbolic price and time are specified: five shekels at the end of the infant's first month. The "*pidyon ha-ben*" ritual is practiced to this day. But another verse hangs unresolved. "Thus says the Lord: Israel is My first-born son." One son in each family is that family's firstborn, but the whole nation is the Lord's. We know how each family redeems its own particular firstborn son. But how is Israel as a whole redeemed? How does the Lord redeem His own firstborn?

The Bible never tells us explicitly, but the answer must be: through circumcision. Firstborns are forfeit on the eighth day, which is also the day on which circumcision takes place. All Israel (the Lord's firstborn) is protected on that deadly-dangerous night of the Passover (when Egyptian firstborns die) by a blood sign—symbolic, ibn Ezra tells us, of the blood of circumcision.

What has our excursus accomplished?[10] Something important for our understanding of the bloodied-bridegroom story. It happens that those verses identifying Israel as the Lord's first-born and threatening Pharaoh's with death *immediately precede* the bloodied bridegroom incident.

The arrangement of this passage is strikingly odd. It demands that we notice and explain.

In verse 19, Moses is ordered to return to Egypt. In verse 20, he takes his family and sets out. Logically the bloodied bridegroom story should come next, starting in verse 21. But it doesn't. It is postponed until verse 24. In between comes the edict threatening Pharaoh's firstborn with death and naming Israel as the Lord's firstborn. These verses are placed where we are virtually forced to trip over them, forced to read our story (which follows them immediately) by their light. The very last thing we hear before the Lord's attack on Moses is a decree that the Lord's firstborn will live, and Pharaoh's will die.

But where does Moses' own son fit? Is he the Lord's first-born, or Pharaoh's?

Thus prepared, the bloodied bridegroom story is a textbook example of an unusual literary genre. It reads like a perfect nightmare. And yet it isn't; it is an actual encounter with God. Once again, encountering God at the end of an inward pilgrimage is just like encountering your own hidden self, and the truth you would rather not know. God waits behind Hamlet's glass.

But instead of seeing a vision as he did at the burning bush, Moses is caught up in a vision; a nightmare vision. To find God on an inward pilgrimage is to see yourself from outside, from God's absolute vantage point—with all comfortable lies and self-delusions stripped away.

The Bible's eye for (and obsession with) deep psychological truth is uncanny. Moses' wife thinks he is an Egyptian—but he isn't. The Lord knows he is an Israelite, but how could he be?—his young son is uncircumcised. Moses has not done the deed that marks out the Israelite family. And the anxiety of being surrounded by persons you have duped, who may discover the hidden truth at any moment, plays straight to a special terror of Moses.

He is supremely humble—and has the weakness of his virtue. "Who am I, that I should go to Pharaoh?" (Exodus 3:11); "but they will not believe me, they will not listen to me!" (Exodus 4:11); "please, my Lord, I am not a man of words!" (4:10). Moses has the insecurity of a man who knows that he is not what he is taken for; who sees himself as a fake, a phony, a fraud. He has duped his wife (who thinks he is Egyptian)—and Pharaoh's enforcers—and maybe the Lord Himself. What circumstances could be more perfectly calculated to trigger a nightmare? Especially at an "overnight stopping place" or "inn" where (naturally!) one sleeps and dreams.

Related but separate, translucent layers are superimposed to make our story, with its striking depth and richness. The idea of God seeking to kill Moses is borrowed from Pharaoh's having sought his life: "When Pharaoh heard of the thing, he sought to kill Moses." Pharaoh and the Lord are quasi-counterparts or antipodes in Moses' career. Yet Moses understands at the same time that the real reason God is angry has to do not with a concealed body but with a concealed identity—with the omitted circumcision. In one compact scene, God reveals His anger and Tsipporah her shock.

As befits a nightmare, the action is confused but the underlying emotions are perfectly intelligible. Moses is terrified of God's anger, anxious about his wife's reaction, painfully conscious of having failed in his duty—and still fretful about that shallow grave he left behind in Egypt. As the burning bush is a perfect summary image of Moses' hidden passion and his whole personality, God's attack and Tsipporah's response are a perfect summary image of Moses' hidden fears at the moment he sets out for Egypt.

Does the Bible describe a nightmare, or a waking vision, or a real event? Maimonides in the *Guide* classifies all biblical stories of this sort as visions or dreams. The Radak agrees with him in most such cases. But the only thing that matters in the end is that Moses is made to confront the truth—a truth, moreover, of surprisingly general significance.

Who would have thought that a story this arcane would bear a message to the Jewish nation at large? But our story, although it presents a deep, sharply focused, highly specific view of Moses' inner life, is also an admonition to all Jews everywhere. For Moses hid something that many Diaspora Jews have been tempted to hide at some point or other. Many have been tempted to call themselves Jews when it is convenient, and Gentiles otherwise.

Encountering God at the end of an inward pilgrimage means encountering the truth about yourself, however hard you have tried to hide it.


There are other Bible stories—dream stories—in which God speaks explicitly from within man's mind. Jacob's dream of the ladder to heaven is one. And there are Bible stories in which man argues with God, who occasions angry and bitter denunciations. "Will You *actually*," demands Abraham, "sweep away the just with the wicked?" "The Judge of the whole earth not doing justice?" (Genesis 18:23, 25). "Shall one man sin," Moses and Aaron ask, "and You rage against the whole community?" (Numbers 16:22). This ongoing argument with God is one of Judaism's most important explicit themes; it appears throughout Jewish history. The Bible combines both themes—the dream story and the waking argument—in powerful inward-pilgrimage stories where man's struggle with God is a struggle with himself.

We find one such story in Genesis 32, where Jacob receives the new name "Israel" and Israel's history begins. Jacob is on his way home—whence he had run for his life, as Moses does much later. Decades ago Jacob had tricked his dying father Isaac into giving him the blessing meant for his elder brother Esau. Esau had been crushed; had resolved to kill Jacob. Returning home at last, Jacob is guilt-ridden and afraid. He has wronged Esau and (even more shamefully) his dead father. "Jacob was very frightened, and in anguish." He prays desperately: "Please save me from my brother's hand, from Esau's hand." After bedding down, he gets up again restlessly and moves his household across the Yabbok river or "ford." And then, "Jacob was left alone."

What should have happened that night to frightened, guilt-ridden Jacob? A good night's sleep? More likely struggle, with himself—with his guilt and fear; with his suppressed inner knowledge; with the truth about himself and his past that he hates to confront. And Jacob does indeed spend the whole night, "until daybreak," struggling with a mysterious attacker. Jacob, like Moses, is an actor in his own vision.

Who is his opponent? Maybe a man, maybe God; the story cannot quite bring him into focus. "A man struggled with him until daybreak"; but later Jacob says, "I have seen God face to face." We do know that at first (as Rabbi Naftali Tsvi Yehuda

Berlin emphasizes in his commentary), Jacob is overwhelmed; but at the end he has the upper hand. It's a hard fight, and Jacob gives it all he's got.

It is this fight that gives Israel its name, which the Bible takes to mean "Struggler with God"—and understands as an honorific. Jews are obsessed with God, and are fighters who will take on anyone, up to and including the Lord Himself. Marcus Aurelius, Roman emperor and philosopher, had a simple view of Jews: "isolated, fierce, and stubborn"—in Matthew Arnold's paraphrase. (Arnold was a nineteenth century English scholar and critic.)

As for Jacob's struggle, commentators ancient and modern are at a loss. Who is this mysterious opponent, and why does he fight with Jacob? When Jacob himself demands the answer, his attacker responds: "Why this asking about my name?" (Jacob seeks but the name remains hidden.) Commentators have proposed angels, aroused spirits, local daemons (e.g., Nahum Sarna's *Genesis*, 1989; several midrashic passages identify the opponent, significantly, as *Esau's* guardian angel). But the text mentions no angel, no spirit, no daemon—just "a man" and "God." Robert Alter is surely right in his Genesis commentary (1996) that "Jacob's mysterious opponent is an externalization of all that Jacob has to wrestle with within himself."[11] Once again the story *shows* us a psychological confrontation instead of merely telling us about it. It shows us Jacob struggling with a physical embodiment of his own psyche—of his own emotional and psychological state. Once again, this epiphany is also a theophany. Once again a biblical hero finds God and his true self simultaneously. And again, he doesn't have a vision; the vision has him—as if he were being envisioned, not envisioning. "*On ne doit pas dire, je pense, mais, on me pense*"; "one should not say 'I think' but rather

'I am thought,'" wrote Rimbaud—who was drowning in his own vivid nightmares.

But Alter neglects the single most compelling piece of evidence for his case. Before Jacob fled from home twenty years earlier, his last guilty act had been—what? To extract a blessing. Most blessings in the Bible are freely given. But this blessing had been meant for his elder brother, and Jacob had tricked his blind, failing father into conferring it on the younger brother (Jacob) instead of the elder (Esau). Two decades later it is the night before his return home, and a mysterious assailant asks Jacob to let him go: "Release me, for the dawn rises." And Jacob says: "I will not release you unless you bless me" (Genesis 32:27). Once again, he extracts a blessing. (Rashi, followed by the Ramban, suggests that when Jacob demands a blessing he is asking, in effect, that the long-ago blessing meant for Esau be made legitimate.)

Sleepwalking Lady Macbeth, making as if to wash her hands, reenacts the night of her sin and crime. Jacob too reenacts his sin. He extracts yet another blessing. The repetition of this act (but this time done rightfully instead of sinfully) makes a strong connection between Jacob's night of struggle and the source of that mental anguish the struggle embodies.

Jacob's is no phantom struggle; it is as real as Lady Macbeth's, as real as a struggle can be. God leads man into the dark wood of his own self: a large implicit theme of the Bible; an explicit theme of the *Torat ha-lev.*

"Long is the way / and hard that out of Hell leads up to light."

Understanding the Bible requires that we understand the dream as a literary genre—one of the richest, most intriguing, and least understood of all genres. Freud took dreams as his text; in *The Interpretation of Dreams* (1899), he gave us a reading of his own dreams as a guide to dreams and dream thought in general. My topic is different: not the dream as we each experience it but the dream as a literary form—which, like the epic poem or romance or Psalm or sonnet, has its own logic and raises its own expectations. A narrative in dream form isn't intended as a transcription of an actual dream (nor does a first-person narrative record, necessarily, the author's own experience). But our experience of dreaming allows us to enter into a dream form narrative, just as our alert, waking life equips us to follow a rational story. We might speak of dream form literature as we do of (for example) the ballet. Both art forms have rules, conventions, and characteristic gestures that guide their departures from the ordinary. In ordinary life, events have rational explanations for the most part, and are not accompanied by music or attended by a corps of dancers. Images are far more important to dream and ballet than to conventional narrative.

The subject is too large for a full-fledged discussion, but it's hard not to notice that the great Czech-Jewish author Franz Kafka (1883–1924) composed mainly in dream form. Here I turn aside briefly to make clear that dream form narrative is no ad hoc invention designed only for reading the Bible.

That Kafka's greatest works cohere only when they are understood as dream form (not rational) narrative is the most central, obvious truth about them. In fact it is so obvious that many Kafka critics never bother to mention it at all. Yet Kafka himself spoke of "the dream-like life of my soul," and his work is so vividly true to all we know about dreams that, beyond a certain point, we stop using dream form to understand Kafka and start using Kafka to learn about dreams. Understanding their genre can't explain these complex texts, but it is a necessary first step—like getting the clef and key signature right when you read music.

In most of his stories, the mood is that vague-but-persistent unhappiness or "dysphoria" that cognitive psychologists find is typical of most dreams. One scene transforms itself into another; characters enter, disappear, and are forgotten; the spotlight wanders as new facts replace old ones; scenes elaborate themselves just insofar as the narrator turns his attention to them; the main character's goals and motives change as the story slips and slides forward as if it were walking on sheet ice in a gale. We meet all these characteristics in our dreams.

Often Kafka's narrator can't quite make out what is happening. ("The verger started pointing in some vaguely indicated direction" [*The Trial*]; "a noiseless, almost shadowy woman pushed forward a chair" [*The Castle*].) Strange events are noted matter-of-factly. (One morning, Gregor Samsa "found himself transformed into a gigantic insect" [*Metamorphosis*]. "Nobody knew where to bury him for a while, but in the end they buried him here"—under a table in a tea shop [*In the Penal Colony*].)

There are many other Kafkaesque examples equaling dream form. Kafka was not the only modern writer to use this form, but he was its greatest master. His work reminds us of the (largely unrecognized) importance of dream form to literature—and especially to the literature of the Jews.

"You should dream more, Mr Wormold. Reality in our century is not something to be faced" (Graham Greene, 1958).[12]

The God of Judaism is often said to be a God of history. The implication is that He broods over human deeds like a chess player and that, although His reasoning might be inscrutable, His will is somehow expressed in His moves. He is said to be "manifest" in history.

This view is wrong. If God (as a certain Jewish physicist once said) does not play dice with the universe, He does not play chess with it, either.

In Maimonides' thirteen principles of faith, no principle asserts that the Lord is a God of history; no principle asserts that God directs history or is manifest in history.[13] Jewish literature, taken as a whole, says just the opposite.

Although the contemporary theologian Eliezer Berkovits does believe in a God of history, the limitations he imposes on the idea make his reservations clear. He points out that, in its simplest form, the "God of history" was a Christian theory (although Christianity has long since dropped it). After all, Christians triumphed and prospered over the centuries while Jews suffered. But long before the advent of Christianity, Berkovits writes, Jews had developed a more sophisticated understanding. They knew perfectly well that you cannot read history as a series of divine judgments on human behavior.

"Yet will I reason with Thee," says Jeremiah to the Lord; "why does the way of the wicked prosper?" Jeremiah had no illusions about the brutal realities of history and human life. A remarkable Talmudic anecdote (Gittin 56b) describes the study house of Rabbi Yishmael, where a verse from Exodus was recited in altered form: instead of, "Lord, who is like Thee among the mighty [*elim*]?" they asked, "Lord, who is like Thee among the silent [*ilmim*]?"

We need only accept the implicit message of these and many other passages to see that Jews do not and could not believe in a "God of history." Could the world's most savagely tormented people possibly believe that God—"gracious and compassionate, long-suffering and full of loving kindness" (Joel 2:13, quoting Exodus 34:6)—is "manifest" in their history? Impossible. And to say that God *is* manifest in history, but in some way we cannot fathom, makes no sense. "Manifest" means "evident to the senses." If God is manifest but we cannot see or sense how, then He is not manifest: QED. The words of the prophet Zechariah are a standing rebuke to all those who expect God to reach into history and forcibly rearrange the pieces: "Not by might, not by power, but by My spirit, saith the Lord of hosts" (4:6).

In Judaism, God's influence on this world is (by His own choice) strictly indirect. He speaks from inside (from the soul, from the human center) to each human being who cares to listen; He is the master whispering advice to a chess player who might or might not pay attention. Whether the master's influence filters through to the chess game itself is in the hands of the human player who makes the moves.

God's withdrawal from history is acknowledged by Judaism as a theological and historical fact. The Temple in Jerusalem was destroyed in 586 B.C.E. It was rebuilt, but the Ark of the Covenant was gone forever. At the start of the Second Temple period, prophecy came to an end. The Talmud tells us that "When the last prophets—Haggai, Zechariah, and Malachi—died, the holy spirit ceased in Israel." The Second Temple was less holy than the first; it had no ark (or ark cover, or cherubim) and (according to the rabbis) no Shekhinah; God's presence was gone.

Yet the Second Temple *was* dazzling, especially after Herod rebuilt it in the first century B.C.E. Although the prophets and the rabbis after them taught that holiness and good deeds are more important than animal sacrifice, they were impressed despite themselves. "He who did not see Herod's temple," the Talmud reports, "missed seeing the most beautiful building in the world" (Sukkah 57b). Meir Ben-Dov agrees; writing "on the basis of the finds uncovered in our archeological investigations," he calls it "the greatest temple of all times."[14]

The Roman historian Tacitus, no friend of the Jews, reports on a war council shortly before Rome's legions broke into the city of Jerusalem in 70 C.E.: "It is said that Titus," the commanding general, "who called the council, declared that the first thing to decide is whether or not to destroy the Temple, one of man's consummate building achievements . . . renowned as one of the greatest products of human endeavor." Some Talmudic authorities even suggested (Z'vachim 118b) that the divine presence had been part of the Second Temple after all. When the high priest pronounced God's holy name in the Temple, the Talmud says, his voice used to be audible all the way to the distant city of Jericho (Yoma 39b).

After the Romans destroyed the Temple in 70 C.E., the silence was awful. What next? Another crucial Talmudic statement answers: "From the day the Temple was destroyed, the Holy One Blessed be He has nothing in His universe but the four *amot* of halakha alone" (Berakhot 8a). Four *amot* (or "cubits") is the space conventionally occupied by one human being. God, in other words, has nothing in His universe but the body and soul of the Jew. The Lord no longer dwells (even symbolically) in the Temple. The Maharsha taught that, after the Temple's destruction, any Jew who studies Torah takes the place of the entire Sanhedrin. The Lord dwells on earth in the living body of Israel—to the extent Israel still follows the command *lekh l'kha!*—still searches inward along the path of halakha.

When a Jew at the end of a long, hard, inward trek reaches God, he becomes a lantern lit with the Lord's light and helps embody God on earth. Man's personality must be ablaze with God's presence to shed the light it is supposed to shed.

The inward pilgrimage of the Akedah resonates with the thrice-annual festive pilgrimage to Jerusalem commanded by the Torah. Jews from all over ancient Israel and the Diaspora would travel to Jerusalem, to the Temple Mount. Jewish texts always speak of "going up" to Jerusalem. Those ancient pilgrimages echo to this day in the Torah ritual of the synagogue.

The ark is traditionally located on the east wall, or the wall nearest Jerusalem; in facing the ark, we face Jerusalem. In Ashkenazi synagogues, the ark is usually at the top of a short flight of steps. And so worshippers who approach the ark (at important moments in the Torah ritual) literally move upward, toward Jerusalem. In approaching the ark, we reproduce the festive pilgrimage to the Temple in microcosm.

Such "microcosmic pilgrimages" are one more deep echo (in the resonant cave of the *Torat ha-lev*) of the kabbalistic idea of a cataclysmic shattering and then scattering of God's presence throughout the space-time of Jewish history. At festivals Jews no longer converge on a single point; they converge on many, all over the world. But these separate, scattered, miniature convergings all point toward Jerusalem like rays pointing to the sun. (Rays from Jerusalem created these Torah rituals all over the world; now Jews follow the same rays back toward Jerusalem.)

In the end of days, said the prophets, it will come to pass that the mountain of the Lord's house will be established as the top of the mountains, and be exalted above the hills, and all nations will flow unto it. Nations do not yet flow to Jerusalem. But psychologizing moderns trying to crack the code of their own psyches are following (at a respectful distance) the Jewish tradition of inward pilgrimage, which itself grew out of the ancient human tides that flowed to Jerusalem at festival time.

Jews in the modern world played a central role in turning man inward: Freud above all, but also such novelists as Marcel Proust, Franz Kafka, Hermann Broch; philosophers such as Henri Bergson, Ludwig Wittgenstein, Simone Weil. The science journalist Richard Panek notes (in his book *Invisible Century: Einstein, Freud, and the Search for Hidden Universes*) the extent to which both Einstein and Freud looked to their own minds, dreams, and thought experiments more than to the outside world.

Simone Weil is a literary philosopher I approach with caution; she was born a Jew but neither understood nor cared about Judaism and eventually turned Catholic. Nonetheless, she made this remarkable assertion about the presence of God (or the "absolute good") far outside *and* deep within each human life: "There is a reality outside of the world, that is to say, outside of space and time, outside of man's mental universe, outside any sphere whatsoever that is accessible to human faculties. Corresponding to this reality, at the center of the human heart, is the longing for an absolute good, a longing that is always there and is never appeased by any object in this world."

In the *Torat ha-lev,* God's cosmos is continuous and unbounded; its farthest reaches are the same as its uttermost, innermost depths. In Judaism's view, God is a still, small voice who transcends the universe but acts on mankind not from outside but only from deep within—through the medium of the human mind. If the human will is a breakwater with waves beating on it from the world outside, God is no part of those waves; He is on the other side, the *inner* side of the human will.[15]

Thus the problem of God's justice in an evil world, Leibniz's problem of "theodicy," is in the end inconsistent by its very nature with the Jewish view of God, man, and the universe. For Judaism the problem is not why God allows evil but why *man* allows it.

The Jewish nation's goal is to show by its behavior and demeanor that God is real. In no sense does God's withdrawal from history nullify Israel's election as the Lord's chosen people. Israel is still bound by its covenant: "You alone have I known among all the families of the earth; therefore will I visit upon you *all* your iniquities" (Amos 3:2). By following halakha (which leads man on his inward trek), Jews become a model of godly behavior—*if* they follow it thoughtfully and well. If they reach their goal and brush up close to the Lord's presence, their demeanors show it. You can see it in their eyes as plainly as Israel once saw the radiant brilliance of Moses' face after his encounters with the Lord.

Of course non-Jews can live faultless and holy lives; non-Jews too can make their ways to God's presence inside. But however Israel chooses to live, the whole world can see God's stamp on the Jewish nation. Only God's presence (the world will conclude one day) can explain Israel's behavior, demeanor, and very existence. On that day Israel will fulfill its destiny. "On that day the Lord shall be one and His name shall be one" (Zechariah 14:9).

How do you make an inward pilgrimage? What route do you follow?

You follow halakha, the "way of going."

The thirteenth century commentator Rabbi Jonah ben Avraham: "How can a man be wise enough to understand the

Lord? This is impossible. But we know Him by exercising justice and righteousness, for the Lord is the author of these."

On the day of God's full and perfect emergence from the chrysalis of human history, when Israel will successfully have embodied God on earth—then the way will be open for the messiah. Jews understand that they themselves must bring him. They must live in a way that makes it possible for him to appear. The Talmud tells a story: one day Rabbi Joshua ben Levi discovers the messiah on earth, sitting among the wretched poor at the city gate. The rabbi asks, "when will you come?" The messiah answers, "Today—if you will only listen to His voice" (Sanhedrin 98a).

Why do Jews do mitzvot? To reach the goal of their inward pilgrimage. Once, Jews needed an ordinary map. (Which way to Jerusalem? Follow this road.) Today they need a spiritual map. (Which way to God?) Halakha is the spiritual map. By following it thoughtfully, Jews put the Lord on earth; they transform Him from a subjective presence within the mind to a manifest, objective fact. "Therefore you are My witnesses, says the Lord, and I am God" (Isaiah 43:12). A startling midrash comments: "When you are My witnesses, I am God. But when you are not my witnesses, I am *not* God—if one may say such a thing." Unless you are My witnesses, I have no presence on earth.

Granted you may strike out on an inward (or any) pilgrimage with no map at all—and perhaps even reach your goal. But for those who want a guide, halakha is it. For those who want to be part of God's presence on earth, halakha makes you part of it—if you follow the law for its own sake, for the love of God.

Each Jewish child is born with this duty: by playing his part as a Jew among Jews, to make God manifest on earth; to make God an objective reality.

The contemporary thinker Michael Wyschogrod reminds us of the Bible's idea that Israel is the Lord's "dwelling place"—and goes on to assert that God is in some sense "incarnated" in the nation of Israel. But to embody God on earth is not Israel's inheritance or birthright, it doesn't happen automatically; it is Israel's duty, its mission, its goal. Jews undertake the labor and struggle of inward pilgrimage to reach God, confront God, *know* God and themselves. If embodying God were merely an inherited status, a matter of the right genes, you could no more become Jewish than you could become beautiful, brilliant, or bald simply by choosing to be. To be born a Jew is, rather, to be born with heavy duties and special knowledge. If you are born a non-Jew you can assume the duties, master the knowledge, and become a Jew—and join Israel's mission.

God's withdrawal from history into the human mind was a momentous transition, symbolized by the transition from Ark to ark—from the Ark of the Covenant in the First Temple to the holy ark in every synagogue today. At the Temple, God's presence on earth was "centralized" or "concentrated" in the Holy of Holies. (But the rabbis compare the Holy of Holies to a cave by the sea: when the cave is flooded the ocean's level remains, to our eyes, undiminished. If God fills the Holy of Holies, His presence in the rest of the cosmos is likewise undiminished.)

Later the Lord was present wherever God-fearing, halakha-following persons made Him present, or allowed His presence to emerge.

And here we finally arrive at a tentative answer to the overwhelming question: why did God withdraw? Why should God no longer reach into history, and why should He never do so again until the messiah comes?

We can't answer, but we can try.

Maybe God withdrew so that mankind could grow up.

A loving parent faces no greater or more painful trial than setting his children free to make their own ways in the world. (Judah, regarding his youngest brother Benjamin: "The boy cannot leave his father; if he left his father, then his father would die" [Genesis 44:22].) For a loving God to allow mankind to grow up—and Israel especially, the Lord's "first-born"—is a remarkable piece of divine abnegation, an unparalleled act of love. No other religion understands God to have permitted a transition so profoundly difficult yet necessary.

For God to assume (or resume) the power to rearrange the world from outside would require a fundamental transformation. Jews hope fervently for just such a transformation—in other words, they hope for the coming of the messiah. This *is* an article of faith, one of Maimonides' thirteen. But Jews also believe that it is mankind's responsibility, not God's, to cause this transformation and bring the messiah. (Remember Rabbi Joshua ben Levi's encounter at the city gate.) In fact, they believe it is *their* responsibility, the Jewish nation's.

True, they often wish and sometimes pray for things to be otherwise. (They long, in a sense, to be children again.) The eminent Talmud scholar and Holocaust survivor Rabbi David Weiss Halivni cites one part of the Rosh ha-Shanah liturgy as "uniquely characterizing" Jewish prayer in Nazi death camps. It is a passage imploring God to "rule over all the world in Your glory"[16]—begging Him, as Halivni puts it, "to take the reins of government back into His hands."

It is the "ultimate tragedy of history," writes Eliezer Berkovits, that God must hide Himself and permit cruel injustice to exist. But more likely, the "ultimate tragedy of history" is not God's sometime silence but man's coming-of-age. And it is not

all tragedy. Many sorrows but (also) many consolations accompany growing up. As with persons, so with nations. God's
withdrawal from history (the end of prophecy, the destruction
of the Temple) is balanced by His upwelling within each human
being.

And God abandons no one. He offers spiritual and not
physical help—but help that is real nonetheless, as real as help
can be. Any man can approach God by imitating Abraham at
the Akedah and answering *hineni,* "Here I am"—and then by
following Abraham, Jacob, Moses, Elijah down the path that
leads inside.

When Israel came of age it was forced to leave home, by the
Roman legions who put down separate rebellions in the first
and second centuries C.E. The Diaspora had long been a fact
and there were important Jewish communities abroad; but
henceforth (and until the rebirth of the Israeli state in 1948),
the promised land was no longer the Jewish homeland except
spiritually. Yet even in the bleakest moments of the Diaspora,
the land of Israel was never just a childhood home reluctantly
left behind. Love and longing for Zion is the irreducible minimum of the Jewish religion.

Some Jews believe that Zionism is a secular alternative to
Judaism, a last-ditch pseudo-religion for Jewish-born atheists;
an emergency life preserver for the Diaspora in an era when
Judaism proper has lost its buoyancy and saving power. In fact,
Zionism is the part of Judaism that can survive a temporary
loss of faith in everything intangible and spiritual. (Zionism
can itself be spiritual, but it can also represent the simplest,
gut-level demand for fairness and justice.) Zionism holds Jewish minds in alignment within a powerful force field, awaiting
the day when Judaism itself can return full-force.

But remember that Zionism proper is part of Judaism. To be a Zionist is to be a Jew. In the end the phrase "secular Zionist" involves the same contradiction as the phrase "atheist Jew." It was Judaism that kept the Zionist fire burning not for a paltry eight days (as in the miracle of Hanukah) but for two millennia. Thousands of years ago an encounter with God created an explosive brilliance so great it still lights the Jewish landscape. That encounter created Jews, Judaism, and Zionism. Zionism can stand alone in the short term, but only Judaism in full can sustain the Jewish people and their state for generations to come.

The inward pilgrimage, central theme of the Bible, leads you to God and your own self.

Goethe understood the pain of not knowing who you are; of having buried the truth too deep to be found, of having heaped too many lies on top. In *Harzreise im Winter,* a poem later set to music by Brahms[17] in his unearthly beautiful *Alto Rhapsody,* Goethe wrote:

> But who is that, wandering alone?
> He loses his way in the brush,
> behind him the branches
> close back together,
> The grass springs back into place,
> emptiness swallows him.
>
> Ah, who can heal the pain? . . . secretly he wastes
> his own virtue
> in useless self-searching.
>
> Is there in your Psalter,
> Father of Love, one melody

that can reach his ear,
and revive his heart?[18]

For Jews, that one melody is the Lord's still, small voice. As they make their ways steadily toward it—a hard trip!—halakha helps keep them from getting lost. Observant Jews know (for the most part) who they are and what they are about, because God knows.

An inward pilgrimage has two connected goals, or one goal with two facets: to reach yourself and your God. We have discussed the consequences of "reaching yourself"; but reaching your goal means knowing God too. What happens when you succeed?

Eliezer Berkovits knows that this goal can be reached. He proves it in *With God in Hell: Judaism in the Ghettos and Death-camps* (1979). Jews who were trapped in the Nazi death machine sometimes resolved to fulfill the commandments no matter what it cost them, as well as they possibly could—although they were absolved of this responsibility, in the extremity of their suffering, by Jewish law itself. But they did not choose to be absolved. In the jaws of Nazi hell, with Nazi teeth grinding them, they followed the inner way to God, the way of halakha, seeking strength from the Lord; and they were strengthened. This is no sentimental theory. It is historical fact.

Berkovits writes about a survivor of the Lodz ghetto who noted "how the Torah teachings of his father and other pious Jews helped him cope with continually mounting suffering." The survivor's comment: "Perhaps now some will believe me when I say in full truth and seriousness that to this day I have not tasted life as I did in those days of trouble."

Another survivor writes about the murder of Shlomo Zlichovsky, hanged for no cause on the eve of the festival of Shavuot, which celebrates the giving of the Torah at Sinai. Shlomo Zlichovsky died reciting *sh'ma yisrael,* proving "in the presence of all these oppressed Jews . . . that the German hangmen have no power whatsoever over the Jewish soul." And the narrator cited by Berkovits continues: "The next day, after the hangings, I joined a secret minyan that assembled in our house for the festival service. We received the holy Torah with joy and fervor and sang the *Akdamut* [a hymn for Shavuot] to the tune of Shlomo Zlichovsky that was vibrating within us." (Is there in your Psalter, Father of Love, one melody that can reach his ear?)

One story, representing many, was reported by a Jewish *kapo* at the Plaszow camp:

> As the camp commander took a number of young . . . Hasidim to be put to death, one, Israel Eisenberg, asked for permission to say a few words of farewell to his friends. I stood opposite them and heard every word. He did not speak many words. He said to his friends that they should rejoice because they were going to die for *kiddush haShem . . . kiddush haShem* [sanctification of God's name]. He got hold of the hands of another *bahur* [young man] and started singing. They were calling to each other: "The most important thing . . . let us rejoice!" They all began to sing and dance as if a fire had been lit within them. Their sidelocks, which till then were hidden under their hats, they now pulled out and let them hang down their faces. They paid no attention to what was going on around them. They were dancing and singing. And I thought I would lose my senses . . . that young people should

go to their death as one goes to a dance! Thus dancing, they jumped into the pit as a rain of bullets was
pouring down on them.

Many Jews who were trapped in the Shoah unquestionably said, with the Psalmist: "God has forgotten, He hides His
face, He will not see, *ever*" (Psalms 10:11). Many undoubtedly
said, "My God, my God, why hast thou forsaken me?" (Psalms
22:1). They had every right to say so. But some who sought God
did find Him. Nothing in the whole literature of mankind
speaks so vividly of God's reality. No other witnesses say as powerfully as these that God lives, and halakha is a way to reach Him.

Kant's God, the "God of the philosophers" par excellence,
is distant from man, untouched by prayer; is merely one term
in a metaphysical equation. The God sought by desperate tortured Jews in Nazi death camps, whom they begged for help,
who answered their prayers—that is a God whose existence
Kant never suspected.

It is true that Jews have no idea what God looks like or is
like, but they know He is near and that He answers prayer. And
if you should say: I prayed for this or that and didn't get it, my
prayer was not answered, Judaism responds: that you were *able*
to pray is the answer to your prayers; some day, perhaps, you
will know it.

That still, small voice you hear: is it the genuine voice of God,
or merely the human stirrings of your all-too-human mind?
The image you have arrived at: is it a sign (like the burning
bush) of God's presence? Or only a strange dream?

The Bible knows that sometimes it is hard to tell. Listen
once more to the story of Elijah at Horeb. First came the wind,
and "the Lord was not in the wind." Then came the earth-

quake, and "the Lord was not in the earthquake." And after the earthquake, fire, and "the Lord was not in the fire." And finally a still, small voice. The parallelism of the text makes us expect a phrase to follow, but it is missing. The text does not say that the Lord was in fact in the still, small voice.

Is it God's voice? When "the Lord called" to the child Samuel, who grew up to be a great prophet, the boy ran to the priest Eli and said: "Here I am, since you called me." It can be hard to tell, even for prophets-to-be. "An honest religious thinker is like a tightrope walker," writes Wittgenstein. "He almost looks as though he were walking on nothing but air. His support is the slenderest imaginable. And yet it really is possible to walk on it." Judaism's way is never the easiest, and is often the hardest.

A Jew might search for God inside and fail, even repeatedly. But when he does fail, he can never lose contact altogether. I've mentioned the religious centrality of certain phrases, such as *sukkat shlomekha* (the shelter of Your peace) and *tahat kanfei ha-Shekhinah* (beneath the wings of the Shekhinah); but these are more than merely evocative and moving. They have been spoken reverently for many centuries. They have been burnished over the generations, like the stones of the Western Wall. But they are no mere objects. They are words or disembodied voices speaking of God. Two other examples, familiar in Hebrew and English: the three-part priestly blessing ("May the Lord bless you and keep you . . .") and the twenty-third psalm ("The Lord is my shepherd"). This last example spans a great cultural canyon: the Hebrew words are often sung to a characteristically Jewish melody (sad and hopeful, hopeful and sad) at the end of the Sabbath, and the lovely King James translation is known throughout the English-speaking world. Passages such as these have the power to change the state of mind and soul. When a failed seeker is chilled to the bone by sadness, such phrases make the sky glow and warm the chill, if only for a moment. In a sense these passages are "angels," mediating between man and God, bearing messages from the Lord even when we cannot discover any sign of His actual presence. (Those who search for angels that the modern mind can understand are deceived if they expect to find them in the forms imagined by medieval painters.)

The way to God cannot be easy. For Jews it can be especially difficult. Yet this strange Jewish nation, famous for skepticism, always reserving its right to doubt, cannot shake religion out of its hair; is haunted always by the *Torat ha-lev*. Jews insist on their right to condemn God vividly, violently, to doubt His very existence—and to take their complaints straight to God. ("Will You *actually* sweep away the just with the wicked?") In their unending conversation with Him they insist that they are not sure He exists; they deny Him in language whose every word implies their belief in Him. Ultimately they can no more deny the Lord's reality than their own, because He is part of them. Their mission is to put God on earth, to make Him manifest, to embody Him in the nation Israel. "When you are My witnesses, I am God, but when you are not My witnesses, I am not God." Their goal is to make God real on earth; on that day the Lord will be one and His name one. On that day Israel itself will be the veil between man and God, and God will wrap Himself in His own people as in a tallis—*if* one may say such a thing.

The deepest, most moving expression of the Jewish art of affirming by denying is in the Talmud—in a famous passage (Menahot 29b) in which the rabbis imagine Moses and God in conversation. God has just shown Moses a vision of Rabbi

Akiba martyred, hideously torn to death by the Romans. This is a moment of crisis at the very heart of the rabbinic enterprise, a whirlpool at the ocean's center. Moses asks God in anguish: "Master of the Universe, this is Torah? And *this* the reward?"[19] All God can answer is, "Silence! That too has occurred to Me." Sometimes, the Talmud concedes, even God cannot believe in God.

This passage from Menachot throws one more (one last) powerful spotlight on God's having withdrawn from history into the human mind. To see how, consider Rabbi Akiba and[20] Jesus of Nazareth.

Akiba and Jesus both taught the love of God and man, sometimes in nearly identical words—for they were both Jews who knew Torah. Both believed in the messiah's imminent coming: Akiba believed that the Jewish revolutionary leader Bar Kokhba was (or might be) the messiah. Both had enemies in the Jewish community, and far more dangerous enemies among the Romans. Both were martyred—bestially tortured to death—by Rome. Each man's martyrdom became a central event to his religious community. (Akiba's death *al kiddush Ha-Shem* is retold every year on Tisha b'Av, the darkest fast day of the year, and on Yom Kippur, the holiest.) But Judaism and Christianity reacted to these two martyrdoms in decisively different ways.

For Christians, the martyrdom of Jesus was part of a divine plan. God put Jesus into Miriam's womb for just this reason, and the Romans who murdered him (and the Saducees who turned him over to the Romans—*if* they turned him over to the Romans) were all playing their parts in a preordained plan. (The Saducees were literalist, legalist defenders of the Temple cult against their great antagonists the Pharisees, who argued for a broader, deeper Judaism. The noble Akiba was a quintessential Pharisee.)[21] The Christian reading of the Passion is accordingly *the* paradigm example of "God in history" thinking. It is the perfect illustration of the argument that says, "In the events of history, we see God's hand."

No Jew, on the other hand, could possibly argue that God *intended* for Akiba to be tortured to death—that God wanted it that way; that this barbaric act was part of God's own plan for history. So profoundly alien is such a reading to Jewish thought that the Talmud, envisioning God's response to Akiba's martyrdom, comes within a hairbreadth of blasphemy. The Lord is so moved, so grief- and horror-stricken when He recalls that terrible scene—so far is it from anything He could possibly have wanted or planned—that He is almost stunned into speechlessness ("Silence! That too has occurred to me")—*if* one may say such a thing.

How can we possibly argue that Jews see God as "manifest" in history?

Of course, Israel's prophets *did* see God in history, albeit long before the end of the Second Temple; thus Isaiah (for example) refers to Assyria as a rod in the Lord's hand, threatening divine punishment against the godless Jews. And Isaiah's advice to the kings of Judah, when they are faced by the deadly Assyrian threat, is to do nothing and trust in the Lord.

But this advice was rejected by Jewish kings of Isaiah's own day, and by later groups whose allegiance to Judaism was unquestionable. It was rejected by the Maccabees in their revolt against the Seleucid Greeks, rejected again by Judaean patriots (or zealots) in the war against Rome that culminated in the Second Temple's destruction in 70 C.E., and again by Rabbi Yohanan ben Zakkai when he took the crucial step of founding a new Torah school in Yavneh—so that Jewish learning would continue in the land of Israel despite the ruin of Jerusalem. It was rejected again by Rabbi Akiba when he endorsed Bar Kokhba's rebellion against Rome, which ended with defeat at Betar in 135 C.E. By no means do such bold actions speak of lost trust in the Lord, as some scholars have argued; none would have happened had the actors not believed deeply in God and His Torah. But these events *do* say that to wait passively for the Lord to act (as the Israelites were required to do, for example, at the Red Sea) no longer jibes with God's relationship to history as Jews understand it. A new idea of man's own responsibility is reflected in the most famous of Hillel's dicta in Mishnah Avot, which—although Hillel was a profoundly pious Jew—do not mention God. "In a place where there are no men, strive to be a man." "If I am not for myself, who will be? If I am only for myself, what am I?" "Do not separate yourself from the community!"

God in His love allowed the Jews to grow up.

The atheist responds: why say that God *used* to be manifest in history, *used* to be "out in the open" during man's childhood but has since hidden Himself in the human mind? Aren't you saying merely that man *used* to be ignorant? That in his primitive state he thought he saw God, but when his understanding matured, he knew better?

Allow Wordsworth to respond, in the famous Ode in which he recollects his earliest childhood. "There was a time when meadow, grove, and stream, / The earth, and every common sight, / To me did seem /Apparell'd in celestial light, / The glory and the freshness of a dream." He tells us (in other words) that as a child he saw differently, saw *more,* than he is able to see as a grown man. "It is not now as it hath been of yore;— /

Turn wheresoe'er I may, / By night or day, / The things which I have seen I now can see no more."

Is the poet telling us that his mind used to be primitive but has since improved? Was the greatness of vision he knew as a child merely delusional? Is he retailing false memories? Recalling things that never were? Of course not; the young child's greatness of vision was real. And the countless readers who have experienced the same truth in their own lives have made the "Intimations Ode" one of the most treasured poems in English.

A small child's vision is not merely broader or deeper than ours; it takes in a dimension that adults cannot see at all: "celestial light, the glory and the freshness of a dream." To become mature is to experience a sort of dimensional collapse— as if you had once lived in a three-dimensional world but are now confined to a plane, and have become a two-dimensional creature yourself. In fact the dimension we have lost is not "the third dimension," and this is no science fiction story; we have lost the "celestial" dimension, the one that makes possible a direct awareness of God. Wordsworth writes, "Trailing clouds of glory do we come / From God, who is our home: / Heaven lies about us in our infancy! . . . At length the Man perceives it die away, /And fade into the light of common day."

Judaism sees the growth and maturing of the Jewish nation in a broadly similar way. Men did indeed encounter God during the nation's childhood. Hard-bitten atheists may choose to regard those encounters as psychological rather than historical facts, but in no case can they be dismissed as invention, delusion, or manifestations of primitive thought. Wordsworth explains that we must grow up, but must lose something precious in the process—something whose remembrance we (wistfully) treasure.

Biology used to have a theory, long discredited, called

"recapitulation," or "ontology recapitulates phylogeny"; a developing embryo was said to recapitulate each stage in the development of the species itself. The analogy between Wordsworth's view of infancy and Judaism's of national infancy is superficially similar but in fact unrelated: it is an observation relating the intellectual and spiritual development of a particular nation to the experience of one poet (and of those who recognize their own experience in his). It is no theory or law of biology; it is, instead, an observation about microcosms and the shattering-and-scatterings that recur in Judaism. To approach the *aron kodesh* in synagogue is to make a pilgrimage to Jerusalem in microcosm. The festival pilgrimage still exists in the form of countless microcosmic pilgrimages scattered over space and time; the spiritual evolution of the nation still exists in the form of countless individual experiences scattered over space and time.

"The fool hath said in his heart, There is no God" (Psalms 14: 1). Today the atheist publishes a book about it. Such an atheist is like an emotionally frigid philosopher who says in his heart, "there is no love in the world." Should he wish to change this apparent state of affairs, he need only love someone and accept love in return. But if he chooses not to, he must understand that he has made an assertion not about the world but about himself. If *you* see no God in the universe, striving to make yourself holy (or godly) will change your way of seeing. "Ye shall be holy, for I the Lord your God am holy" (Leviticus 19:2).

Of course, there is a difference between personal perception and objective reality. To bring God's presence to earth, or rather to bring it *back* to earth—to bring His presence out of the mind, back into everyday reality—we begin by leading godly lives; but no one person can achieve this cosmic goal by

himself. The idea that God is "incarnated" in the Jewish people
seems to me (as I have said) wrong; the reality is subtler, and
admittedly harder to grasp. The Jewish nation as a whole is *potentially* an emergent system. When all Jews strive at last to be
holy, the nation will become an emergent system in fact. And
what will emerge? God's presence on earth, the Shekhinah itself. That mist over the lake, that inscription in the mosaic is
not imaginary but objectively real, and God's presence on
earth will be too—"if you will only listen to His voice."

Is it good or bad to have God inside you, and spend your life
struggling toward Him like Abraham toward Moriah? "In every
single generation," the Passover Haggadah says, as I have noted,
"they rise up against us to destroy us." Then it adds—with bitter irony because it is false?—or plain bitterness insofar as it is
true?—"and the Holy One Blessed be He saves us from their
hands." So long as Jews exist, God is *potentially* present on
earth—and Jews will suffer for it. The Jewish nation marks the
site where God is not but will be. Jews are the four silent letters
that will one day speak God's name. They are the dark rose
window with a sun shaft creeping slowly up behind. They continue to struggle into themselves to obey the command, *lekh
l'kha:* go inside!

To recapitulate, beginning with our questions:

> How can we accept the simultaneous existence of a
> just, all-powerful God and a merciless world? If God
> is omnipotent, why does He not act to stop injus-
> tice? Aren't we forced to conclude, from the fact that
> He doesn't, either that He doesn't care or doesn't
> exist?

God as Judaism understands Him speaks to every human being in a still, small voice—an inner voice. The role He has chosen in this world is to act not *on* but *through* mankind; to act not from outside but from within.

No one argues that it is easy to locate and heed this inner voice. Jacob's all-night struggle with his mysterious antagonist, which at first he seems to be losing, is a metaphor for every Jew's struggle with himself—with lostness and hopelessness, with the world at large and with his own occasional (even frequent, even habitual) inability to hear that small and quiet voice. Abraham's terrible journey to Moriah is a metaphor that hits even harder. But in bad times we know, at least, that the voice does speak and can be heard, if only we can track it down; and we console ourselves with the sanctity that halakha imparts to every moment of life. Halakha sets life to music; gilds time itself with holiness—which is sometimes the color of blood.

Why should God have done it this way? And why should we grow up, and (if we are lucky) watch our children grow up, and be required to set them free? At least God offers powerful consolation to his firstborn: when the moment comes at last when the Jews, somehow, both hear and heed that divine voice within them ("*Hear,* O Israel," they exhort themselves twice every day), they themselves will become the veil, or the tallis—if one may say such a thing—of the living God.

# VI
# David's Dance

We are left with four images as we circle the city of Judaism. From the north, the Torah scroll held high and wide open, to the sound of rushing water; from the east, a large tallit by itself, and the sound of a shofar; from the south, a man and woman embraced ("Let him kiss me with his mouth's kisses!—your love is better than wine," Song of Songs 1:2) as someone blows out a lamp; from the west, Abraham's face at the moment he catches sight of Mount Moriah, to the sound of a still, small voice—rustling satin, or the long sigh (faint cymbals) of ice-covered branches trembling in a breeze. Then we close our eyes and look again, and all four images have been consumed by a burning thornbush and the snap of flames. The images are sharp, as in Jacob's or Joseph's dreams; this book itself is written in a kind of dream form.

We need our religious traditions because we are part animal and part angel, matter *and* mind; in a world that supplies all our animal and material needs but none of our spiritual or

ethical ones, we spin, crash, and burn like an airplane with a
wing torn off.

Jews need Judaism because they are more at peace and
feel better when they have done right than done wrong, when
they have acted generously than when they have acted meanly,
when they have done their duty and not ignored it; and at
times they need to pull free of the tighter-and-tighter vise of
physical existence and go higher, if only for a moment. But
they know also that life is God's greatest blessing and we must
savor it, not toss it down and ask for a refill, or a glass of something better. They know that we ought to reject Baudelaire's
famous invitation to treat life like cheap liquor (*Enivrez-
vous!*); instead we ought to taste it, and achieve not drunken-
ness but joy.

But if we don't know what's right we can't do it, and can't
reach the state of calm joy that follows. If we don't know our
duty we can't do that. Not knowing what is right, what is our
duty, and which way sanctity lies is the greatest cause of unhappiness in our Western world today. To deprive human beings of that knowledge by rearing them ignorant of religion is
not to set them free but to make them miserable—and unable
even to say why they are unhappy.

Judaism tells Jews what is right, and what is their duty. "It
has been told you O man what is good, and what the Lord requires of you: only to do justice, love mercy and walk humbly
with your God." Hillel adds: "If I am not for myself, who will
be? If I am only for myself, what am I? If not now, when?" Jews
know that Judaism is right because it is a living thing built of
lapped lives, a 3,000-year-old tree with its roots thrust deep
into sacred time and its branches still growing and in bloom.
But it never asks that you submerge your identity in the common cause. It invites you instead to join your own people, who

want you. Judaism is your family seated at table asking you please to join them, not stand at the door; not walk away.

Will you join them?

And bring your children. To Judaism the idea of a Jewish parent with a non-Jewish child is bizarre if not incomprehensible. Judaism is a religion of parents and children together. "These words that I command you this day, lay them to your heart," says the Lord; "and teach them to your children."

The Talmud describes fathers walking up to the Temple in Jerusalem with their children on their shoulders: a familiar picture of father-and-child closeness two thousand years old.

Judaism tells Jews what is right—and adorns the bare thread of human life with sanctity, jewel-by-jewel, until a Jewish life glows with soft color: warm amber and silver, cool fragrant yellow and glowing orange and translucent purple-rose. Of course such a life can be hard. Abraham struggling three days through a blasting storm of anxious pain toward Moriah is, not for nothing, a metaphor of Jewish life. Moses pushing on year by year through the desert and the near-unmanageable throng that almost drowns him, dying at last at the brink of his destination, is another metaphor. Yet for thousands of years Jews have found the prize worth the price. Judaism is above all a religion of joy; *the* religion of joy. Will you join in?

I've argued that to understand Judaism you must see it whole. You can't grasp such a rich structure in a single view, any more than you can know how Jerusalem (or the U.S. Capitol) looks from a single photograph. Nor can you grasp Jerusalem whole from a pile of pictures, each of a different detail. But if you are given a group of photos and each one shows the whole city from a different angle, *and* you put them all together in your mind—then it is possible that you may grasp the city as a whole, or at least be able to guess what it is like.

I have tried to present Judaism as a whole by describing four image-themes, each a microcosm of Judaism or (in other words) a view of it all from one angle. All of Judaism is present in "separation," and the "veil," and in "perfect asymmetry" and "inward pilgrimage." You can put these images together yourself, superimposing (at least) four translucent images that form an "emergent system"—more than the sum of its parts. And you will have noticed that each of my four thematic images is built, itself, of many superimposed elements, and that many of these elements ("separation in time," for example, which is part of "separation," which is part of the whole) are themselves many-layered. The structure I've described is "recursive," to borrow a term from mathematics and computing: the same structure recurs at many scales, on many levels.

This bouquet is made of flowers gathered from all over time. And one more image: Judaism is a sea. Each phase of Jewish literature adds translucent ideas to an ever-deepening pool, with the Bible at its base. We read the Bible *through* the Talmud as if through translucent stained glass. Seeking to understand Judaism on the basis of the Hebrew Bible alone without the Talmud makes no more sense than trying to understand Christianity on the basis of the Hebrew Bible alone without the New Testament. (And despite their radically different worldviews and theological conclusions, there are certain similarities between the New Testament and the Talmud.) We read the Talmud in turn through centuries of commentary that have accumulated around and upon it. The latest works of our own generation appear on top. It is all one sea of Torah—dive in and explore any level directly, or gaze downward from above into the depths of an ever-deepening literary and religious tradition.

A student pushing off from shore and swimming out into this vast sea for the first time ought to know Kierkegaard's description of the "religious sense"—it is like "always being out alone over seventy thousand fathoms." Those who have swum in a calm bay or a clear, deep, quiet pool meant for diving know the exhilarating, unsettling experience of being safely supported over a huge wide-open space beneath you.

Is there more to be said about my four microcosmic theme-images?

"Separation" implies the doctrine of man's transcendence. Man is not part of nature; is defined over and against nature. He must struggle out of and away from nature, toward God; must struggle out of nature like a baby struggling to be born (or a figure by Michelangelo struggling out of rock—a struggle the artist represented often by leaving his blocks of marble partially uncarved). This struggle is the meaning of holiness, and of man's search for transcendence. It is all implied by one statement of Torah: man is made in the image of God. That one phrase annihilates paganism; for pagans, the gods are made in man's image—and the natural end-point of paganism is man worshipping himself. But for Jews, man is modeled on something incomparably better, and must therefore struggle not to perfect but to transcend himself: to be braver, nobler, more loving and forgiving, more just and honorable than he would otherwise ever think of being.

Jews defy nature by defying its most fundamental impulse—the deadly onrush of chaos, reducing all things to one level, abolishing all distinctions. In this theme-image, the forced-apart waters of Creation become the upright water-walls at the split-open Red Sea, which become the upright standards of the rolled-open Torah scroll in synagogue, and the forced opening of birth itself.

Separation is life; holiness is halakha.

To the outsider, halakha seems complex and arbitrary.

But it has a unifying theme, which applies to kashrut and family purity, Sabbath and festivals, kiddush and havdalah, planting land, weaving cloth, making marriages. The theme is separating, in space and time.

Why live by halakha? Because the Jewish law gilds time with sanctity, creates *sukkat shlomekha,* the shelter of God's peace—and lets you stand with your people, not just watch from the audience. An Orthodox Jew is a rigorous observer of halakha in every detail, but to do even one mitzvah well is a first step, and a better step than doing them all badly. Halakha grows and changes—but adjustments are made (and can only be made) by *talmidei hahamim,* those who are learned in Torah and Talmud and the rabbinic tradition. Changes cannot be decreed by amateurs, kibitzers, or scholars learned not in Torah but in something else.

In this sense halakha is rigid. But Judaism is not rigid. It welcomes those who are partially successful, partially observant—so long as they don't claim that the commandments they do not or cannot observe are non-commandments and have been (conveniently) canceled. The Passover Haggada begins with this passage: "Here is the bread of affliction that our fathers ate in the land of Egypt. All who are hungry, come and eat! All who are needy, come and join in the Passover." This invitation is essential Judaism: if you are in need, physically or spiritually, join us and be sustained.

Second, the "Veil"—which implies the doctrine of God's transcendence. What the world calls Judaism is only a reflection in a window. You cannot see through the window, because the far side is black (or at any rate, invisible). But you must grasp that it is a window, that there *is* a far side—and the far side is God. God is transcendent: cannot be seen, described, imagined. All you can imagine is the windowpane. All you can know is that it *is* a windowpane.

Yet the God of Judaism is no cold, remote abstraction— thanks to this windowpane, thanks to the veil itself. Jews believe in a transcendent God who does not part the veil to become human but does invite (indeed implore) man to approach. The veil proclaims that God's ineffable, transcendent presence can be closer to you if it is separated from you. You cannot see or know God but you can see, know, and approach the veil, knowing that God is on the other side. The veil symbolizes God's inconceivableness and (simultaneously, paradoxically) draws God and man close.

In this theme-picture, the veil is the tallit worn at prayer, the mask Moses wears after encountering God, the two veils of the Holy of Holies, the curtain before the holy ark in any synagogue, the opaque tefillin boxes or the mezuzah hiding biblical texts; the Ark of the Covenant, screened by cherubs' wings, hiding the tablets of Sinai. The veil is present in the wordless, tuneless cry of the shofar, the overpowering blank of the Western Wall, and a Jew's refusal in all circumstances to pronounce God's proper name. These phenomena seem widely dispersed, and studies of Judaism do not ordinarily group them together. But in the *Torat ha-lev* they are separate layers of one deep image.

Why is the omnipotent, transcendent, and one-and-only-one God of Judaism no cold and remote abstraction? Because you can approach the veil as close as you like, and know that the Lord is just on the other side. The veil can be soft as cotton on your face.

Third, "perfect asymmetry" and the bride—which implies the doctrine of man's twoness and (by association) inductive morality.

God is one but man is two: not male or female but male and female. Husband and wife create a whole man out of two halves. Their sexual union is inherently blessed whether or not a child is engendered. In Judaism, the cult of the couple has given to marriage a supreme and unique importance.

In Judaism, male and female are perfectly asymmetric. (A Jew and the land of Israel have a similar relationship: they fit together and create a new unity. Fertility is important in both cases.) The force field between maleness and femaleness creates marriage and colors the whole universe. But the modern attempt to make the two sexes interchangeable, shorting out the battery that operates civilization, wiring its poles together, is an act of aggression against both sanctity and humanity.

The purpose of life is to marry and rear a family. (The question of happiness is broader.) Another modern idea, that career and not family is the point of life, is un-Jewish—and for Jews it is therefore wrong. Because man cannot exist except where male and female are one, the Jewish "self" is a strange, unfamiliar self inhabited by two separate beings, two separate I's. In Judaism the basic dichotomy is not Buber's "I and thou" but "we and Thou"; and the self that includes another person is a hint or foretaste of a self that includes God.

Jewish morality is inductive. It starts with the ground case and works outward. You approach the goal step by step. It is no accident that the verse in Leviticus does not merely say "love thy neighbor" but "love thy neighbor as thyself." You know how to begin—namely, with yourself; now, move forward. The ground case (love yourself) is your basis for the inductive expansion (love your neighbor). It's true that loving yourself doesn't always come naturally; "I never found man that knew how to love himself," says Iago in Shakespeare's *Othello*. (And he is an expert at self-regard.) But self-love comes closer to being a universal human trait than any other kind of love.

Philologists and Bible critics once thought they were scoring points off Judaism by arguing that, in "love thy neighbor as thyself," the word "neighbor" refers not to "fellow man" but only to a member of your own group or tribe. But this is a glory and not a weakness of Judaism. Judaism gives us a method for approaching goodness. (Many have noticed that those who are filled with abstract love for all mankind tend to be the least loving of people in practice.) All things considered, it's easy to love yourself; and most people find it easy (thank God) to love their families. From Leviticus it follows directly that, in Judaism, self-love is *required;* otherwise you are failing in a religious duty. Self-love and love of family, of your own flesh and blood, supply practice and experience in what love entails—which make it possible and even natural to love a wider circle in a gentle, un-dramatically expanding fashion, like an outward-rippling circle in still water.

Is Judaism bigoted against women? No. Male and female are different in body and mind, but each is basic to man's being. The doctrine of man's twoness is inherent in the Bible's first chapter: "And God created man in His image; in God's image He created him; male and female He created them." Male and female are man's basic elements. In chapter two, Eve is *k'negdo,* "directly encountering" her husband, "eye-to-eye with him." The assumption that women must do just what men do or be doomed to inferiority *ipso facto* betrays contempt for women and womanhood—and puts man on a pedestal. Normative Judaism has no female rabbis, but women are invited to learn as much Torah (in the broadest sense) as they like. And in Judaism, learning is incomparably more important than performing for the crowd.

\* \* \*

Finally the "Inward Pilgrimage"—which implies the doctrine of inner listening and, along with it, the religious legitimacy (in fact, inevitability) of doubt.

If you look for God in history, you will not find Him. The problem of evil is man's problem; the central question is not why God hasn't saved the world but why *you* haven't. Jews accept God not like children who look to their parents for miracles but like adults who pull their share, who freely accept *ol malkhut shamayim,* the yoke of heaven's kingdom—the duty of being a Jew. To find God, Jews try to find the "still, small voice" that the prophet Elijah heard: the echo of God's own voice, an *inner* voice that is sometimes (too often) impossible to make out, lost in the static and the pain, but present nonetheless.

After the destruction of the Second Temple in 70 C.E., after Bar Kokhba's revolt against Rome some six decades later, the Jews were driven out of their homeland and a remarkable thing happened, unprecedented in human history. Jews never wanted to, never planned to—but they left home and grew up.

This is where modern Zionism originates. The land of Israel is a Jew's home. People sometimes say about farmers that they are "attached to the land," which is wrong; they are attached to *their* land. To say that a farmer is merely attached to the land is like saying that a happily married man is attached to the Female. Jews are attached to Zion, *their* land, the land of Israel.

But why should Judaism be connected to some particular strip of ground on a small planet in an out-of-the-way solar system?

The answer lies in another question: what does it mean to be happy?

The first psalm replies. *Ashrei ha'ish,* it begins, "happy is the man" who does not sin, who delights in Torah; "he shall be like a tree planted by streams of water, that bringeth forth its fruit in its season." To be happy is to be planted. To fit, belong, feel rootedness as firmly as you feel dry cool earth between your toes, to bring forth your fruit in due season—to achieve what you were meant to. Zionism says symbolically that, as a man must be married to be whole, he must be planted to be happy. (True, some are not destined to be whole, some are not destined to be happy, and all are destined for bitter sorrow and disappointment. They are invited to be Jews nonetheless.)

Historically Zionism served another purpose, too. Jews have arrived, today, at a time for going home. But two thousand years ago it was time for coerced departure. "To every thing there is a season, and a time to every purpose under the heavens" (Ecclesiastes 3:1). With the collapse of the Second Jewish Commonwealth during the 1st and 2nd centuries C.E., Jews were forced to leave home. Israel's spiritual and material supports were gone. In the black sobbing ruins Jews looked around and discovered they were on their own. Had God abandoned them?

No, God had not. He had only moved inside. Henceforth, He dwelled within Israel; Israel was God's tabernacle. God was no longer the maker of fires, storms, and earthquakes; He was the inner voice. Israel had depended on God and always would. But henceforth God would depend on Israel too. Having been created, reared, and protected by God, Israel would now show what it had learned and what it was worth. Israel the land where God (metaphorically) dwelt became Israel the people where God (metaphorically) dwells. Throughout the long Diaspora Israel would show its devotion to its Creator—and to its childhood home.

Zionism is the universal human wish to return home to the place where you were a child and safe; where (as Wordsworth wrote in a passage I have already cited) "The earth, and every common sight, / To me did seem / apparell'd in celestial light, / The glory and the freshness of a dream." More than that: Zionism stands for an impossible world in which children love their parents and want to go home as much as parents love their children and want them back. Zionism stands for the world imagined by the very last prophet in the last two verses of his book: "Behold I will send you Elijah the prophet" says Malachi—"and he shall turn the heart of the fathers to the children, and the heart of the children to their fathers" (4:5–6). This is where prophecy ends; henceforth God speaks only to each individual separately.

The idea of the Jews' (and by analogy all mankind's) growing up is a basic religious principle, too. How could a just God permit this evil world to be? But Judaism tells us an obvious yet startling fact: "*lo ba'shamayim hi,*" the Torah is not in heaven; it is on earth, is mankind's to interpret and apply and enforce. And another startling fact: "From the day the Temple was destroyed, the Holy One Blessed Be He has nothing in His universe but the four amot of halakha alone." God has nothing in His universe but those human minds that accept His commandments.

And from that point on, from the day the Jews left home, to locate God a man must pull himself nearly inside out, must discover and expose to himself his own identity—and will reach God finally right at the center, at the mid-point of the vast and imposing rose window of the mind and soul and self.

Conscience, the devil once said, is a Jewish invention; and he was right. But doubt is part of Judaism, too. The Bible and Talmud are records of the Jews doubting God and God doubting the Jews and the Jews doubting themselves and (in one famous passage in tractate Menahot) of God doubting Himself.

But for a Jew the path is clear: doubt, but act. Doubt God, but do what He tells you.

The *Torat ha-lev* is a book that is hardly free of its own paradoxes, as readers will have noticed. Separation from man and the crowd leads to union with the Jewish people and with God. Vivid awareness of our apartness from God (*there* is the veil that separates us) leads to vivid awareness of God's nearness. Historical separation from God—the Temple's destruction and the experience of *galut*, Diaspora, leaving home—points a way back to God by plunging into one's own self, and creates (ultimately) a Zionism in which the Jewish nation grows up and returns home older, wiser, wounded to the heart and yet ready and able to do its duty in this world. (The Maharsha taught that the Messiah was born on the day the Temple was destroyed.) "In a place where there are no men, *you* strive to be a man." Man must be holy, therefore separate—yet "it is no good man's being alone"; and when he finds a mate he finds God, too.

Paradoxes and all, these are my four themes. They show the Jewish people coming to terms with nature, God, history, and man, and together they make a partial and preliminary version of the *Torat ha-Lev*, the mind-and-heart Torah that records those ideas that emerge from Judaism as a whole.

I return, at last, to an assertion I made earlier—that Judaism is above all a religion of joy; is *the* religion of joy.

The *Torat ha-lev* is "written" in images, is a collection of images. So what image in this Torah best captures the Jew's relation to the world and to God? Some might answer: the man Moses as the Bible draws him, austerely powerful and sometimes furious, humble yet commanding; used to encountering the Lord of creation and changed utterly by those encounters. Unlike any other man in history.

Moses is indeed the central man in Israel's birth and Judaism's emergence. But he is not Judaism's emblem—though its real emblem is also biblical. It is David in a linen ephod dancing ecstatically before the Ark of the Covenant as he leads it into Jerusalem.

And David danced before the Lord with all his might; so David and all the house of Israel brought up the ark of the Lord with shouting, and with the sound of the trumpet. (II Samuel 6:14–15)

This image symbolizes better than any other the essence of the Jewish attitude. "Thou wilt show me the path of life: in thy presence is fullness of joy" (Psalms 16: 11).

Maybe we can see best how David's dance stands for Judaism if we glance aside at the emblem of Christianity. There we find another Jew, tortured to death by the lowest kind of barbarian. For Christianity this moment represents, also, the highest and most exalted type of service to the Lord—and Judaism cannot disagree; Jews mourn their martyrs intensely. But Psalm 100 begins with these verses that are quoted in the prayer book: "Shout unto the Lord all the earth! Serve the Lord in joy, come before Him in song." Sabbath observance in synagogue begins with a sort of fanfare, sung triumphantly: "Come let us sing to the Lord! Let us shout to the Rock of our Salvation!" (Psalm 95). Judaism's emblem must encompass both these passages.

We honor and mourn our martyrs, but Judaism in the end is celebration—and defiance. Those are the underlying colors of Jewish life. Jews celebrate nature but defy it; will not be part of it. They celebrate history but defy the seemingly unsolvable problem of theodicy that history poses. They celebrate sexuality but defy it to turn them into animals. They celebrate God, ineffable and transcendent—but defy God's unknowable transcendence to awe them into silence, or keep them at a distance, or stop their constant arguing and questioning. Their duty is to go forth like Abraham and be God's tabernacle on earth, to give *God Himself* (no less) a local habitation and a name.

Judaism is a building (temple, palace) that shows a blank and inscrutable face to the street. My goal has been to lead you to the inner courtyard or garden, which is invisible from outside. How do we get there, and what do we see when we arrive?

We get there through a long, dark, cave-like passage. The cave itself is another recurring image in Judaism.

The legendary cave with Rabbi Shimon inside composing the Zohar is a defining image; it is the nutshell with infinity inside. ("I could be bounded in a nutshell, and count myself a king of infinite space," says Hamlet, "were it not that I have bad dreams." But Judaism's dreams are not bad. They are dreams of the world's salvation.)

The cave is symbolized by the oldest surviving synagogue in Europe, the Altneuschul in Prague. The building dates roughly from 1280, although parts are older. The insides of medieval churches are centrifugal, drawing the eye outward toward windows and sculpture and arcaded aisles and monuments and side-chapels; dead center, beneath the crossing, is usually empty. Synagogues are centripetal, directing the eye inward toward the bimah at the center, where the Torah is read in the midst of the congregation.

The Altneuschul seems strikingly cave-like inside, narrow and tall and full of soft dusty light. Its grave beauty and whispery grandeur are striking; the inside is densely decorated with metal grillwork around the bimah, hanging lamps, carved wood, the golden-red banner presented by Charles IV in 1368, an elaborate menorah, the ark. A perfect image of Rav Shimon's cave: an inner infinity, separate from the world, where the mind travels inward toward God without stopping.

The cave is also a symbol of the *Torat ha-Lev;* of the interior Torah that remains invisible to the outside world. Postclassical Jewish civilization developed as if in a cave. Cut off from everything irrelevant and external, it blossomed with fantastic profusion. Illegible to outsiders, it was profound and beautiful to those whose eyes had adjusted to the strange soft light. The *Torat ha-lev* seems like a blank page at first; but the longer you look, the more you see. It describes Judaism's profuse stillness, when the exterior world goes blank—and the inner world explodes into dazzling brilliance.

In Prague, one of the old seats along the rim of the Altneuschul is marked as the Maharal's place—the seat of Rabbi Yehuda Bezalel Loewe (1525–1609). In later years a folktale about a mysterious man-made Golem appropriated Rabbi Loewe as its hero (just as Rabbi Shimon bar Yohai had been appropriated as the author of the Zohar). This Golem, a kind of giant automaton, came to life and became a defender of the Jews only when the rabbi slipped into its mouth a paper inscribed with the four Hebrew letters of God's name. Otherwise it only *looked* like a man.

Why has this folktale always seemed so inevitable and so right to Jews? Because they know (at least subliminally) that *they* are the slip of paper bearing God's proper name. They would be mere coarse clay themselves without the Lord's presence inside. And they were created for no other purpose than to make the coarse clay of humanity come spiritually alive; to make it man.

But let us return to that cavernous passage. What do we see in the end, when we have walked its whole length and emerged into the light of the innermost courtyard at last? Do we find a mysterious empty cloister, silent, where stillness reigns and God is near? Unlikely. What we see in fact is tumult, jubilation, ecstasy. Unbounded joy. David's dance.

Jews don't decorate their synagogues with the dance; instead they re-enact it. (In Judaism, our own lives are the medium in which we work.) The Ark of the Covenant no longer exists, but the text of the Covenant is written in the Torah. By parading triumphantly with the Torah, as we do every week, we re-enact David's dance. By dancing with the Torah, we create an even better, truer version—and we dance this way every year on the festival of *Simhat Torah,* "Joy in the Torah." On that evening and again in the morning, we make seven circuits around the synagogue, carrying with us every Torah the congregation owns—usually two or three at least, sometimes a dozen or more—with banner-waving children mixed into our noisy, singing, disorderly procession. I have seen frail, elderly Hasidic rebbes dance like crazy men on *Simhat Torah.*

What do we find at the center of the vast, intricate, beautiful palace that is Judaism? Joy in the Torah; joy in the Lord; David's dance. A thread of ecstasy stretching all the way from that long-ago dust-choked Jerusalem morning to this very day and onward into the future, until the coming of the messiah—the whole world, space and time and suffering and all, pulled together by triumphant jubilation; by David's dance; by joy.

"Those who sow in tears shall reap in gladness."

"Not by might, not by power, but by My spirit, saith the Lord of hosts."

—New Haven, May 2009: Sivan 5769, *Erev Shavuot*

# Appendix A:
# Why Believe in God?

This is a book about Judaism, which presupposes the existence of God. Discussions about God's existence—whether or not one can prove it, and, if so, how—are unnecessary to an exposition of Judaism's basic themes. But it seems wrong to sidestep the question.

It seems especially wrong in view of my insisting, in Chapter 3 ("Veil"), on God's ineffable, intangible transcendence. The sacred veil of the *Torat ha-lev* is opaque. You "sense" God's presence on the other side, but that is only a metaphor; you cannot see, hear, or (literally) feel God through the screen. The screen is blank. So how do you know that God is there? How do you know He exists at all? And if you don't or can't know, why believe in Him?

Here I deal with that basic question.

Although we have been living for generations in the age of atheism (or so it has seemed), this atheism often turns out to be shallow—professed uncritically and without thinking. Its fundamental tenet is that our ethical principles are merely reasonable, and useful, and obvious, and therefore require no transcendent source of authority. But those principles are not merely reasonable, they are not self-evidently useful, and they are certainly not obvious.

Nor are they merely the preferences or whims of one particular culture (namely ours). Saying "I prefer that no one be tortured to death" is not like saying "I prefer orange juice for breakfast." It reflects a moral absolute, independent of anyone's opinion or whim or preference. Virtually no serious person denies this.

But let's look at these questions from a slightly different angle.

First: if God exists, how come no one can prove it? Practicing Jews know that God is real, and yet no proof of that fact has ever emerged or ever will.

Why not? The answer is inherent in a statement some Jews make: God's existence is something I perceive, like the blue of the sky. I can see the sky is blue, no one has to prove it to me; and God's reality is equally a matter of perception, and equally one where the idea of "proof" is inapplicable.

In other words, some people perceive God to be real; others plainly don't. Those who perceive Him do so on the "inside"; they perceive His presence within them. And things you perceive in your own mind—your mental states—cannot be transferred to anyone else. They are "subjective." No proof for God exists or ever will, because—in our age, anyway—God's reality is a subjective and not an objective fact.

I don't mean that God is real only for some people, or exists only for those who perceive Him. God is real for everyone. In arguing that God's reality is subjective, my goal is to suggest how God's existence can be real, yet not subject to proof.

God exists for everyone and everything in the universe—and exists independently of this and all other universes. Yet I say that His existence is a "subjective" fact because of Jewish teaching, and because of what I observe. Judaism teaches that God is outside this and all other universes (is transcendent) and is inside every human being (is immanent). These facts are contradictory, because the truth is too big for human language to express or minds to grasp. But insofar as God is outside the universe, we can't go there and see Him. He might act on the universe—but in that case we wouldn't perceive God, only actions or objects we might attribute to God. We do not see God perform the actions or create the objects; we only infer that He did.

Of course, our ancestors in the ancient past reported miracles that could only have been God's work. We don't anticipate seeing any ourselves, but we have every right to believe our ancestors. God was an objective fact for them: many people could see and believe the same direct evidence. But there is no way in which placing trust in our ancestors can transform God from a subjective to an objective fact for us. We believe their reports, but there is no objective reason why we should.

God is also present inside man (as I have argued in Chapter 5, "Inward Pilgrimage"). Which again makes His reality subjective. No one else can see or sense what is inside your mind: it belongs to you, is real to you, is true for you—and only you. The God within you is real, but you alone can see and sense Him; anyone else must sense God within himself, not God within you.

That God's reality is perceived or known by believers, not deduced, is often lost on nonbelievers. The distinguished philosopher David Chalmers throws light on this fact, accidentally. "Think of religious beliefs, for instance, or beliefs about UFOs," he writes, "which can arguably be explained without invoking any gods or UFOs. But these are all quite possibly *false* beliefs, and not obviously instances of *knowledge*. By contrast, we *know* that we are conscious" (*The Conscious Mind: In Search of a Fundamental Theory* [New York: Oxford University Press, 1996]). But religious belief is (in many cases) exactly *not* a hypothesis intended to explain certain facts but a matter of perception or simple knowledge—like consciousness itself.

We cannot prove that God exists, yet evidently most people of Jewish or Christian background believe that He does. They have this belief, moreover, even if they don't say or think they do; even if the belief is implicit or subliminal. The human mind is a compass needle that points to God. It doesn't work infallibly; there are damaged and diseased human beings. But it works well enough on the whole.

We can see this human compass needle working when we consider absolute moral values. The following discussion is no proof that God exists; such a proof is (as I say) impossible given the nature of the proposition. I only assert that nearly everyone in modern society *believes* that He exists—including many who call themselves agnostics or atheists.

Here is my argument. Let's suppose you are (and you call yourself) a "reasonable person"; being reasonable, you have "inner promptings" that give you moral guidance. They tell you, for example, not to commit murder. Accordingly you don't. Even if you somehow found yourself in a position in which you could murder in cold blood a person you have every right to hate, in such a way that no one would ever find out—you still wouldn't do it.

So far, there is no need to mention God. There might be all sorts of purely rational or psychological grounds for this inner prompting of yours.

But now suppose you come upon *someone else* who is about to commit murder. For concreteness, suppose the potential murderer has pinned the intended victim underfoot and is about to smash in his head with a sledgehammer. Presumably you would see it as your duty to compel the would-be murderer to desist. Whether you actually do anything would probably depend on a variety of factors: the tools at hand, the presence of others, your own bravery. But you'd *want* to stop the murder, and believe in your right and duty to stop it, whether or not you were able to put this desire into effect.

Now, what gives you the right to compel another person—in this example, a potential murderer—to obey *your own personal* inner promptings?

You might answer that "my inner promptings tell me not only that I personally must not murder, but that I must compel all other potential murderers to desist." But remember: you're a reasonable person. As such, you can't deny that the potential murderer has *his own* inner promptings, which might tell him that murder (or at least this particular murder) is a good thing, or even a mandatory thing. If you insist that your behavior must be governed by your own inner promptings, why shouldn't this other person's behavior be governed by his?

Since you are a reasonable person, your only rational conclusion is that each person has a right to obey his own inner promptings—insofar as they don't collide with anyone else's. And when they do collide with someone else's? You still have no basis for asserting that your inner promptings are right and the other person's wrong (leaving aside the law, which is irrelevant for our purposes). It is reasonable for you to refrain personally from committing murder. It is unreasonable for you to compel others to do the same.

Of course you might invent or borrow a theory purporting to prove that murder must always be forbidden—or must at least be forbidden in the case we are discussing. Still, you are right back where you started: the would-be murderer can develop his own theory, which is just as compelling to him as yours is to you, and (being a reasonable person) you must concede that you have no right to assert that your theory trumps his. Your theory might tell you that it holds everywhere, for everyone; but outside the world of the theory, you are still a reasonable person, and as such you must concede that everyone is entitled to his own theory. (The exact same thing is true if your theory happens to be Kant's celebrated Categorical Imperative, which holds that you must act in such cases as if each action were to be ordained as a universal law.)

But now let's leave reason aside and return to reality. In fact you *would* compel that would-be murderer to stop, if you could. (And you'd do so even if you found yourself in an outlaw state where there was—in effect—no law against murder.) But what gives you the authority to compel the would-be murderer to stop? To compel another person to bend to your inner promptings instead of following his own? What makes it right in your own mind? Not reason. The answer must lie elsewhere.

We know two things about this authority that has given you (in your own mind) the right to act. First, it must hold sway over (or set bounds to the behavior of) every human being on earth—because your wish to halt that murder had nothing to do with the murderer's identity. Second, it must outlaw murder and any other crimes or sins concerning which you believe yourself empowered to act.

In short: unless you are proclaiming yourself supreme and absolute ruler of mankind, you must implicitly believe in God. And not just any God. Most modern, ethically minded people will find their "inner promptings" more or less in agreement with the Ten Commandments and the Holiness Code (Leviticus 19:9–19), as modern theologians and thinkers understand them:

> Thou shalt leave [the gleanings of your fields] for the poor and the stranger. . . . Ye shall not steal, neither shall ye deal falsely, nor lie to one another. . . . The wages of a hired servant shall not abide with thee all night until the morning. Thou shalt not curse the deaf, nor put a stumbling block before the blind . . . in righteousness shalt thou judge thy neighbor. Thou shalt not go up and down as a talebearer among thy people; neither shalt thou stand idly by the blood of thy neighbor. . . . Thou shalt not hate thy brother in thy heart. . . . Thou shalt not take vengeance. . . . But thou shalt love thy neighbor as thyself.

In other words: your belief that you have the duty and authority to stop a murderer before he starts suggests that you believe, implicitly, in the God of Israel.

Notice once again that this is not an argument or proof that God exists— merely that you *believe* He does, whether you know it or not; whether you admit it or not. God's existence is a subjective fact that cannot be proved. But we can show that human nature is a compass needle that points in His direction.

Some intellectuals will go to any lengths to deny this truth, but there has been no way around it since the day Nietzsche (with blazing integrity) parked the trailer truck of his ethics squarely in the middle of modern man's intellectual interstate, blocking the way forward. By acknowledging that to reject God forced him to reject "Judeo-Christian morality," Nietzsche gave the game away. God and absolute morality are inseparable.

To put this in simple but rigorous logical terms: Nietzsche acknowledged that to reject God implies the rejection of Judeo-Christian morality. The truth of a statement of this kind implies the truth of its "contrapositive." If to *reject* God implies the rejection of Judeo-Christian morality, then to *accept* Judeo-Christian morality implies the acceptance of God. Nietzsche saw clearly that, if you want Judeo-Christian morality, you cannot have it unless you acknowledge that the Jewish (or "Judeo-Christian") God is real.

Nietzsche himself followed his own logic: he rejected God *and* Judeo-Christian morality. Judaism, of course, accepts God and rejects Nietzsche's cruel "patrician ethics." Hillel did not say, "If I am not for myself, who will be?" and stop there. He continued: "If I am only for myself, what am I?" Jews do not pray (quoting the Psalm), "May the Lord give strength to His people," and stop there. They continue: "May the Lord bless His people with peace."

Modern atheism, on the other hand, insists that you can close your bank account and keep writing checks. But that is a lie. Without God in the bank, your moral checks are drawn against nothing. It is also a pretense. An atheist who denies God while insisting on the binding absolutes of Jewish morality—which, of course, he will call something else—has in effect proclaimed himself god. We know where *that* road leads.

Why believe in God? To be honest with yourself, and preserve the morality you already accept.

Human nature is a compass needle that points to God. How did the atheist know that it was right to compel a would-be murderer to desist? Not by figuring things out, but by shutting down his ability to figure things out. Reason is an unreliable guide—as any intelligent demagogue can show you; fired-up crowds who do violence have generally been fired-up to ignore, not to follow, their inner promptings. To convince people to do what comes naturally, no demagogue is required. Our atheist knew his decision was right not by reasoning but by listening—for a still, small voice.

# Appendix B: What Makes Judaism the Most Important Intellectual Development in Western History?

Over the last hundred years, world history has tended increasingly to converge with Western history. Western colonialism was a powerful force generations ago, but Western ideas have proved far more powerful. Throughout Asia, such big ideas as capitalism, freedom, democracy, and (modified) Marxism have transformed the landscape—naturally, in different ways, and to varying extents in different countries. In a dangerous inversion of the same process, much of the Arab world's leadership seems unified by hatred of Western ideas (and especially of Israel and Judaism).

My calling Judaism the most important intellectual development in Western history—I might almost have said world history—is not meant to provoke Christians or Moslems or anyone else but to provoke thought. Obviously many will disagree. But too many people have developed (in the name of tolerance) the habit of declining to say who or what is "best" or "most important" in any human endeavor at all—which shows not tolerance but laziness. (In Martin Amis's *House of Meeting* [2007], the narrator speaks of young people: "They're so terrorstricken by generalizations that they can't even manage a declarative sentence. 'I went to the store? To buy orange juice?'") Those who disagree with my judgment should offer their own candidate for "most important intellectual development" and compare. No prizes are awarded for first place. The point of the game is not the decision but the process of reaching it.

Notice also that I stake my claim on behalf of Judaism, not Jews. The Jews themselves, as opposed to the Jewish religion, have not been an unalloyed blessing to mankind. On this point merely consult the Bible, which includes harsh condemnations of the Jewish people. I'll be more specific below.

As for Judaism itself, it has given morals and spiritual direction to Jewish, Christian, and Muslim society, and indirectly to the modern and postmodern worlds. But not only that. Judaism formed our ideas of God and man, of sanctity, justice, and love: love of God, family, nation, and mankind. But not only that. Judaism created the idea of congregational worship that made the church and the mosque possible. But not only that. Much of the modern liberal state grew out of Judaism by way of American Puritans, neo-Puritans, and quasi-Puritans who revered the Hebrew Bible and pondered and cited it constantly.

But not only that. Also this: the best ideas we possess come straight from Judaism.

> "You must love the Lord your God with all your heart, all your soul, and all your might." "You must love your neighbor as yourself." "It is no good man's being alone." "Choose life and live, you and your children!" "The day God created man, He made him in God's image." "Man, it has been told you what is good, and what the Lord requires of you: only to do justice, love mercy, and walk humbly with your God." "Justice, justice must you pursue!" "Man does not live by bread alone." "Do not follow a multitude to do evil." "In a place where there are no men, strive to be a man."

All of these thoughts but the last come from the Hebrew Bible, and the last is from the Talmud. When Jesus is asked, "Master, what shall I do to inherit eternal life?" (Luke 10:25)—in other words, what is the right way to live?—he elicits and approves an answer that combines the first two Hebrew statements cited above. Jesus replies to his questioner: "What is written in the law? how readest thou? And he answering said, Thou shalt love the Lord thy God with all thy heart, and with all thy soul, and with all thy strength, and with all thy mind; and thy neighbor as thyself" (Luke 10:26–27).

Jesus responds in turn: "Thou hast answered right: this do, and thou shalt live" (10:28). Thus, the essence of right behavior as Jesus himself understands it is given in the Hebrew Bible. (See also Matthew 22.)

Of course, the Hebrew Bible includes not only deep truths but assertions we can no longer accept; indeed, in some cases we reject them in horror. The Bible faithfully transcribes the babble of voices and opinions that existed at just that point when mankind was coming morally and spiritually alive. (This assertion says nothing about divine or Mosaic authorship of the Torah; "the Torah speaks in the language of man," say the rabbis, and if God wrote the Torah, it follows that there were no limits on what the text could say or how it might be structured.) But the Bible, as I have said, is not Judaism. The rabbis of the Talmud selected, out of the many doctrines preached in the "biblical academy," some to endorse and develop and others to disregard and (in effect) suppress. Judaism is the structure built by the rabbis on the foundation—the Temple Mount—of the Hebrew Bible.

Yet almost nobody knows Judaism. This unknown land made civilization possible with its spiritual exports, yet the land itself remains a deep, dark mystery except to the small circle of practicing Jews who live there. People used to say that Western civilization stands on two pillars, the Greek and the Hebrew. Judaism is one of those two massive columns in the undercroft of Western civilization—and is all but unknown.

(In Brague's intriguing theory of Europe as a culture based on deliberate borrowings, Christianity is a direct continuation of Rome; Greece served as Rome's primary, authentic source for borrowing, and Judaism played the same role for Christianity. "The Christians are essentially 'Romans' in that they have their 'Greeks' to which they are tied by an indivisible bond. *Our Greeks are the Jews*" [emphasis in the original] [*Eccentric Culture, A Theory of Western Civilization* (1992)].)

People know (for example) that Judaism is ardently nationalist but not that it is fiercely universalist. They know that it is "legalistic" (governed by laws, like American society), but not that it is profoundly forgiving and humane.

The ancient Greeks had a word with no equivalent in classical Hebrew. A "barbarian" babbles, speaks no Greek—is a foreigner and thus inferior by definition. Hebrew has no such word. The biblical *nokhri* means foreigner, but with no connotation except "unfamiliar." And the word *ger* means only "stranger." "The stranger (*ger*) that dwelleth with you," says the Bible, "shall be unto you as one born among you, and thou shalt love him as thyself; for ye were strangers in the land of Egypt: I am the Lord your God" (Leviticus 19:34). The prophet Micah tells us something related: "For all people will walk every one in the name of his god, and we will walk in the name of the Lord our God for ever and ever" (Micah 4:5). Each nation will do as it pleases; as for us, we will worship the Lord.

Given these and similar verses, and Talmudic ideas on the same topic, Judaism developed the idea of universal fellowship among all believers in a basic religious and moral code. The great medieval thinker Menahem Ha-Meiri discusses all persons who "are bound by proper customs and serve

God in some way, even if their faith is distant from ours." Such people, he writes, "are to be considered in exactly the same way as Jews."

Judaism is universal where the ancient Greeks were particularistic, kindly where they were fierce. During the seven days of the festival of Sukkot, says the Talmud, seventy oxen were sacrificed at the ancient Temple in Jerusalem—one for each nation of the world (Sukkah 55b). The Greeks are not known to have offered sacrifices on behalf of Israel. The *Aeneid,* arguably the greatest poetic achievement of ancient Rome, begins, "Of arms and the man I sing." The 101st psalm begins, "Of mercy and justice I sing." That contrasting pair of verses is one way to understand the difference between the two great pillars of Western civilization.

Another example: Judaism is indeed legalistic—and is also the most flexible and forgiving of religions, because God Himself is understanding and forgiving to the last degree. Maimonides writes (in his commentary on the Mishnah, Makkot 3:16) that "even if you perform only one commandment perfectly for its own sake, for the love of God, you qualify for eternal life in the world to come"—no less a reward than the one awaiting a Jew who spends his whole life obeying all 613 commandments perfectly. In his *Aspects of Rabbinic Theology* (1909), Solomon Schechter illustrates the same point by citing a midrash: "God says to Israel, I told you to pray to me in your synagogues; but if you cannot, then pray in your house; and if you cannot do that, pray in your field; and if this is inconvenient for you, pray in your bed; and if you cannot even do that, think of Me in your heart." A sublime view of God, and distinctively Jewish.

Christianity and Islam both welcome converts, but neither is optimistic about a nonconvert's chance of being "saved" or of pleasing God. The Jewish view is different. The Bible knows no one who is more "blameless," more "upright," or a greater delight to the Lord than a man from Uz named Job. Job is tested *because* the Lord trusts him absolutely; as the Ramban notes, God tests only those He trusts. And Job was no Jew. "How do we know that even an idolater who studies Torah is like the high priest?" asks the Talmud. Because, it answers, "the Bible says, 'which if a man do them, he shall live by them.' It does not say priests, Levites, Israelites—but a *man.* Hence you learn that even a Gentile who studies Torah is like a high priest" (Sanhedrin 59a). A midrash has God say to Moses, "Do I care about a person's identity? Whether Israelite or Gentile, man or woman, slave or handmaid, whoever does a good deed shall find the reward at its side." Here is Isaiah (56:7): "My house shall be called a house of prayer for all peoples."

Now for the qualification I mentioned earlier. If Judaism is the most important intellectual development in Western history, and the Jews are the senior nation of the Western world (which is only a matter of historical record), Jews are no angels notwithstanding. It is only fair that we consider this fact too, which puts Jews in the same boat as every other species of flawed humanity.

The worldview created and preached by Karl Marx, whose father was a convert from Judaism to Christianity, reflects (at least in a general way) the prophetic fervor of Judaism—although Judaism has a consistently realistic and nonutopian view of human nature. In practice, Marxism has inspired untold brutal murders and the slow torture of whole nations. It's hard to establish the exact degree of Marx's own guilt for the bloody barbarism of Lenin or Stalin (and their toned-down criminal successors in the USSR), or the countless inhuman crimes of Communist China, Cuba, Vietnam, and many others. Marx himself was no murderer; but he unleashed a catastrophic doctrine on the world. It's also true that many of Lenin's Bolshevik colleagues were Jews, and that Jewish Marxists were influential all over Europe.

Another example, related if less deadly: over long centuries of Christian persecution, Jews developed a natural animosity toward Christianity. Since the Second World War, many Christians have had a change of heart regarding Jews; some have become true and loyal friends of Jews, Judaism, and Israel. (And in fairness, there had always been a certain amount of social intercourse, even friendship, across the religious divide.) But wariness acquired over millennia changes slowly. A nasty problem arises when, in some "progressive" Jewish circles, a lingering fear or hatred of Christianity has mixed with ignorance of Judaism and left-wing hostility toward traditional institutions, especially religious ones.

This toxic mixture has goaded some American Jews into a harshly abrasive (even crusading) atheism, a fevered fervor for social change, and automatic opposition to all public manifestations of Christianity. These particular Jews have helped sink the morals and happiness of modern America. Jews are hardly alone in this crusade, and are rarely the leaders. But they've made impressive contributions. All such divisive and damaging tendencies are far from the tolerance and universalism of Judaism itself.

Once, in biblical antiquity, Jews were under the impression that God was theirs only. But very soon they came to see that a God who is truly *one* must be God of everything: of all humans, and the whole universe, and all other universes. Everything. And if God is one, *mankind must be one*. All must have the right to say, "This is my God." Which in turn has wide-ranging ethical implications. Even today, the aftershocks of this spiritual earthquake are far— far!—from dying out. Isaiah (45:22) speaks for this revolutionary, universal

God: "Turn to Me and be saved, every farthest reach of the earth; for I am God and there is none other."

There is the true and authentic voice of the most important intellectual development in Western history—or very possibly in the history of the human race.

# Appendix C: Jewish and Christian Ethics

In the first appendix I mention Nietzsche's references to "Judeo-Christian morality." He was neither the first nor the last to use this phrase. Many casual observers believe that the underlying ethics of Judaism and Christianity are essentially the same, and that the principal differences between the two religions center on the messiahship of Jesus and the nature of religious law. It is true that, from the perspective of irreligion or antireligion, the ethical teachings of Judaism and Christianity may seem more alike than different. But if you compare the two doctrines honestly and directly, the differences loom large. I have already pointed out (in Chapter 4, "Perfect Asymmetry") their disagreements on sexuality, marriage, and family. Their dispute over the essential character of morality is just as basic.

In the "action morality" of Judaism, you *must judge* your fellow man; this is a strong obligation. Refusing to judge (being "nonjudgmental," in today's ugly cliché) is callous, cowardly, and wrong—although, as Hillel warns, "Do not judge your fellow man until you have been in his place." Understood: a man might judge wrongly; if so, he will have to face the consequences. Those are the responsibilities of adulthood. (Judaism says patiently, repeatedly: grow up. All of Judaism says, loud and clear, again and again: accept the responsibilities of adulthood.) Reflecting on his experience in Nazi death camps, Primo Levi reaches a related conclusion (in *The Periodic Table*, 1975): regarding "the enemy who remains an enemy, who perseveres in his desire to inflict suffering, it is certain that one must not forgive him: one can try to salvage him, one can (one must!) discuss with him, but it is our duty to judge him, not to forgive him."

Why does Judaism insist that to judge is mandatory? One part of the reason (only one) has to do with mental health. Nietzsche explains: "When a noble man feels resentment, it is absorbed in his instantaneous reaction and therefore does not poison him." Unexpressed resentment can turn to poison in the metabolism of mind. The Bible anticipates this sharp observation by outlawing festering resentment. "You must not hate your brother in your heart; you must rebuke yes *rebuke* your neighbor" (Leviticus 19:17).

And you must also defend yourself: your "self" naturally including your family and extended family, possibly your whole nation and spreading uncertainly outward—ever since the careers of Israel's prophets—toward the whole of mankind. Of course, Judaism believes what Isaiah and Micah taught, that in the end of days nation will not lift up sword against nation. But in the meantime, ever-increasing moral maturity means more and not less fighting, more and not fewer wars, as the strong take up the fight on behalf of the weak. In Judaism, pacifism is immoral; it is the co-conspirator of wickedness.

Not so in Christianity. To the critic and philosopher Michael Tanner (1994), "Resist not evil" is one of Jesus's "most impressive precepts," and one that is (naturally) "in sharp conflict with the law"—meaning Jewish law. Why does Judaism nonetheless reaffirm the law and reject this most impressive precept? Because the Bible says, "Choose life and live, you and your children!" (Deuteronomy 30:19).

Early Christianity was associated, as Tanner notes, with a different morality—I'll call it a morality of passion, born of suffering (*passio* in Latin). The morality of passion insists that you must not judge your fellow man and (ideally) must *not* defend yourself, however you define "self." There is support for this passive morality in the New Testament. Respecting judgment: "Judge not, that ye be not judged" (Matthew 7:1). "He that is without sin among you, let him first cast a stone" (John 8:7). "Wherein thou judgest another, thou condemnest thyself" (Romans 2:1). Regarding pacifism: "Whoever shall smite thee on thy right cheek, turn to him the other also" (Matthew 5:39). "Resist not evil" (Matthew 5:39). "Blessed are the meek, for they shall inherit the earth" (Matthew 5:5). These verses rank among the best known in the whole Christian Bible.

In "Blessed are the meek," Jesus is quoting the Hebrew Bible, as he often does—"But the meek shall inherit the earth; and shall be delighted in the abundance of peace" (Psalms 37:11). So the case is not quite so simple as it might seem at first. But it remains true that, by and large, Jewish thinking is not just different, it is opposite. Christianity: "Whoever shall smite thee on thy right cheek, turn to him the other also." Judaism: "If I am not for myself, who will be?" Jewish morality is warrior morality. It is no accident that Abraham, Moses, and David, the Bible's greatest heroes, should all have been described as warriors. It is no accident, either, that Judah Maccabee should have been so frequently cited in medieval Europe as *the* model of a godly and chivalrous knight. Thus King Edward III is described on his tomb in the Confessor's shrine, the most conspicuous and sacred spot in Westminster Abbey, as "BELLI POLLENS MACHABEUM PROSPERE DUM UIXIT"—the Maccabees' equal in martial prowess. Years earlier a traveling monk had praised the king's grandfather, Edward I, as "the most Maccabean king of the English." There are many similar examples.

None of this implies disrespect for Christianity. Let Christians be Christians and Jews be Jews, and someday perhaps (God willing) the two communities will be like a father and son who are wholly different, who have passed through a long, bloody age of conflict in which the son has grievously wounded the father—but have reached a time of reconciliation. And from then on, although they never gush about how much they love each other, they do love and respect each other all the same.

# Notes

## Chapter One:
## Picturing Judaism

1. Henry Chadwick, *Augustine* (Oxford: Oxford University Press, 1986).

2. Medieval art and Judaism are usually regarded as antithetical; and in a way they are. Yet the main façade of Bath Abbey (for example) is dominated by two sculpted ladders on which angels climb, embodying Jacob's dream (Genesis 28:12). At the Sainte Chapelle in Paris, royal showcase for relics and gorgeous stained glass, twelve of fifteen main windows show scenes from the Hebrew Bible. In Canterbury Cathedral, a stained-glass image of the enormous grapes of Eshkol borne between two men on a staff is nearly identical to a long-standing logo of the Israel tourism bureau. The Coronation Chair at Westminster Abbey in London is thought to have been inspired (along with many other European thrones) by the biblical description of King Solomon's throne. Since the tenth century, England's coronation ritual has made the connection explicit: "Be thy head anointed with holy oil: as kings, priests, and prophets were anointed. And as Solomon was anointed king by Zadok the priest and Nathan the prophet." In *Art and Judaism in The Greco-Roman World* (Cambridge: Cambridge University Press, 2005), Steven Fine describes such artworks as mere "Christian visual exegesis of the Christian Old Testament"; many others agree. But of course such "Christian visual exegesis" usually begins with a simple translation, as direct as possible, of biblical word images into visual images.

3. Otto von Simson, *The Gothic Cathedral: Origins of Gothic Architecture and the Medieval Concept of Order* (New York: Pantheon, 1962).

## Chapter Two:
## Separation

1. What does science offer religion? Evocative ideas and images. "Resonance" is an example. Encountering one instance of a theme-image doesn't bring the others explicitly to mind, but *can* set those other memories gently humming just below the level of consciousness.

2. Allen Grossman, "Holiness," in *Contemporary Jewish Religious Thought: Original Essays on Critical Concepts, Movements and Beliefs*, ed. Arthur A. Cohen and Paul Mendes-Flohr (New York: Free Press, 1987).

3. The separation theme is expressed in the Hebrew language, too: the verb for "understand" or "discern" (*biyn*) is defined in BDB as "discern; become separated, be distinct." Discernment means seeing distinctions, perceiving separations. Thus creation requires that you make separations, and understanding requires that you perceive them. Understanding what things are different and why, and what things are the same and why, is the basis of human intelligence. The Hebrew verb *biyn* actually comes from (or is closely associated with) the word for "interval" or "space between": separation is connected to creation *and* understanding. I owe this thought to an observation by the poet Samuel Taylor Coleridge (1772–1834): "the Hebrew word for the understanding, *binah,* comes from a root meaning between or *distinguishing.*"

4. But notice that the Bible uses "create," *bara,* only of God Himself. In the Bible's view (as the critic Northrop Frye has pointed out), man makes but only God creates.

5. This biblical verse seemed nearly inexplicable to some medieval Bible commentators; why should men *want* to dress like women, or vice versa? They were at a loss. A civilization in which men shaved their chests and women built their biceps was beyond their wildest nightmares.

6. Howard I. Levine, "The Non-Observant Orthodox," *Tradition,* Volume 2 (1959). Levine wrote that many Jews called themselves "Reform" because they saw themselves as Jews but did not observe the commandments—the same holds today; but "we can hardly commit a graver error than that of [automatically] categorizing non-observant Jews as 'Conservative' or 'Reform'. . . . It requires courage of a Jew to join an Orthodox synagogue though he is not observant by Orthodox standards. . . . [Such a person] deserves true Orthodox fellowship and encouragement." Still true.

7. Paul Ziff, "The Feelings of Robots," *Analysis,* Volume XIX (1960).

8. At a circumcision ceremony we pray that the infant will enter one day into "Torah, huppah, and a life of good deeds." We make no mention of law degrees, entrepreneurship, or your first $20 million.

9. Thus Nahum N. Glatzer in *Franz Rosenzweig on Jewish Learning* (New York: Schocken, 1955).

10. Translation by Yosef Hayim Yerushalmi.

11. The Zohar begins as a commentary on the Torah, often explaining the text by proposing unexpected, surprising connections. The Zohar itself is best described the same way, by means of surprising connections. It brings to mind the illuminated Hiberno-Saxon Gospel books of the Dark Ages (for example the surpassingly beautiful Book of Kells), and the twentieth century novels of Vladimir Nabokov, especially *Pale Fire*. Each of these works centers on a commentary-in-art (*Pale Fire* is a novel in the form of a commentary) that overwhelms us with a dazzling profusion of imagery, with its sheer imaginative density.

12. This "cognitive spectrum" is discussed in my book *The Muse in the Machine: Computerizing the Poetry of Human Thought* (New York: Free Press, 1994).

13. One contemporary example is Jonathan Rosen's *The Talmud and the Internet: A Journey Between Worlds* (New York: Farrar, Straus and Giroux, 2000).

14. *Time's Arrow, Or, The Nature of the Offence* (London: Jonathan Cape, 1991) is Martin Amis's remarkable story, told backward, of a descent from 1990s America into the black chaos of the Shoah; it was partly inspired by Nabokov's great novel *Ada* (1969), in which time gathers speed as the characters age. The nature of time has always been one of mankind's great obsessions, and Judaism alters the texture of time (a phrase Nabokov uses in *Ada*) while stubbornly setting human effort in opposition to the running down of the universe—strictly on principle, for the immense symbolic value of the project.

# Chapter Three:
## Veil

1. Abbot Suger, the great patron and part-inventor of Gothic art at Saint-Denis in the early twelfth century, makes plain the difference between the Jewish and Roman Catholic ideas of the veil. Suger's theology is expressed "Not by a text but in images," George Duby writes (1976)—and in this respect is broadly similar to the Jewish theology I present in this book. Suger thought of the stained glass in the epoch-making east end of his Abbey Church of Saint-Denis (1144) as a series of veils illuminated by God's presence: "These translucent panels . . . are to him like veils at once shrouding and revealing the ineffable" (Otto von Simson, *The Gothic Cathedral: Origins*

*of Gothic Architecture and the Medieval Concept of Order* [New York: Pantheon, 1962]). But of course these veils are decorated with images of Suger's God. For Suger, moreover, Jesus "unveiled" the truth; one of his windows shows Jesus tearing the veil off the "old law" of the Torah. The implied reference is to the New Testament passages discussed below in which the "veil of the temple" is said to have been torn open upon the death of Jesus. For Suger, "unveiled" means "revealed"; "that which Moses hath veiled," he wrote, Christian doctrine "unveils" (See *Abbot Suger on the Abbey Church of St.-Denis and Its Art Treasures,* ed. Erwin Panofsky [Princeton, New Jersey: Princeton University Press, 1946). *Aguzza qui, lettor, ben li ochi al vero, / che 'l velo è ora ben tanto sottile, / certo, che 'l trapassar dentro è leggero.* "Sharpen your eyes well to the truth, reader, for now the veil is so fine that to pass within is surely easy." For Dante in the *Purgatorio* (8:19–21), veils are obstacles to be overcome. For a Jew, "unveiled" means the renunciation or eradication of the idea of transcendence; to remove the veil means that we see transcendence die away, "and fade into the light of common day."

2. As in Deuteronomy 32:19–20 or Isaiah 45:15. The philosopher Pascal cites this passage in Isaiah apropos the "hidden God" who conceals Himself from undeserving seekers.

3. Many assertions occur more than once in the Talmud (and in the classic rabbinic literature as a whole).

4. Simon Goldhill, *The Temple of Jerusalem* (Cambridge, Massachusetts: Harvard University Press, 2005).

5. The New Testament relates that, at the moment Jesus died on the cross, "the veil of the temple was rent in twain from the top to the bottom" (Mark 15:38; also Luke 23:45, Matthew 27:51). Some Christian thinkers explain that a fundamental separation between God and man was breached at this moment. But Jews understand God and man to have been intimately close always; the "temple veil" symbolizes God's transcendent sanctity and the fact that, despite this apartness, man can be as close to God as to the temple veil, or to the tallit or the Western Wall or the sound of the shofar. Reading critically, Jewish thinkers might agree that, for Christians, the death of Jesus corresponds to a symbolic tearing open of the sacred veil. But the immediate consequence is not that man and God are no longer separate; rather that transcendence disappears. (Like oxygen vanishing into the void when a spacecraft is punctured.)

6. When Steiner writes about Judaism he is nearly always wrong. But he is the sort of thinker we need to hear on this topic: a cosmopolitan author who is at home in the whole world of Western arts and letters and is never afraid to advance bold, strange, even offensive theories. Even more than that we need to hear cosmopolitan thinkers who are at home within Judaism, too.

7. Cited by Michael Fishbane, "Prayer," in *Contemporary Jewish Religious Thought: Original Essays on Critical Concepts, Movements and Beliefs,* ed. Arthur A. Cohen and Paul Mendes-Flohr (New York: Free Press, 1987).

8. Aramaic, which is close to Hebrew but far from Arabic, was the language of everyday life in the Jewish community for many centuries following the Babylonian captivity; small parts of the Bible and much of the Talmud are in Aramaic. So are parts of the prayer book, including the main body of the *kaddish,* the famous doxology that is recited in memory of the dead (and with which major parts of the prayer service and learned discourses conclude).

9. A. Verheul, *Introduction to the Liturgy: Towards a Theology of Worship* (London: Burns and Oates, 1968).

10. In speaking of this "far side," I don't mean (of course) the *sitra ahra,* the "other side" where Jewish folklore locates demons and devils. (Least of all do I mean the 1980s comic strip by Gary Larson, which played brilliantly on life's bizarre improbabilities.)

11. We have no right to tamper with a single note in a Beethoven score; how much less do we have the right to tamper with God's laws.

12. Since biblical poetry is prose poetry, it has another quality: its robust greatness can survive the shock of translation. Bible translations make up a whole family of literary masterpieces in many languages—notably our own. The Talmud, too, could engender an English masterpiece if we gave it the chance.

## Chapter Four:
## Perfect Asymmetry

1. The Song of Songs is important to Christianity also; Origen, St. Bernard, St. Teresa of Avila, and many others wrote about it. Major Renaissance composers wrote settings for the antiphon *Nigra sum,* based on verses from the Song. (The same verses inspired the first of Byron's *Hebrew Melodies,* 1815: "She walks in beauty, like the night.") One of the most fascinating and original discussions of the *Song* and Christianity is the medievalist Paul Binski's exploration of verse 2:14 ("O my dove that art in the clefts of the rock, in the nooks of the wall") and the symbolism of Wells Cathedral's celebrated west front, and of verse 2:1 ("I am the rose of Sharon, the lily of the valleys"), and others, in relation to Becket's shrine at Canterbury Cathedral, with its alternating rose and white columns (in *Becket's Crown: Art and Imagination in Gothic England 1170–1300* [New Haven: Yale University Press, 2004]).

2. The idea one sometimes encounters that David and Jonathan's

friendship (as described in the book of Samuel) was homosexual or had homosexual aspects is silly. True, David sings of Jonathan in his famous elegy
that "thy love to me was wonderful, passing the love of women" (2 Samuel
1:26). But we seem to have forgotten the traditional meanings of "love" and
"friendship." Othello says to Iago, "If thou dost love me, show me thy
thought," and Iago answers "My lord, you know I love you." Later in the same
scene, Iago apologizes to Othello "for too much loving you" (III.3). Of course
Iago is not sincere; but Othello is. There are innumerable similar examples.

3. Henry Fielding knew the score when he made his hero Tom Jones
an exception: the noble Tom no longer loves Molly (whom he has seduced),
"but compassion instead of contempt succeeded to love."

4. The excavations that are yielding remarkable new views of David's
Jerusalem, to the south of the Old City's walls, are the most exciting arche-
ology in the world today.

5. The marriage ceremony in classical Athens centered on the following exchanges. The bride's proud father: "I give this woman for the procre-
ation of legitimate children." The bridegroom: "I accept." The bride's father
proclaims the amount of the dowry. "I am content," says the husband. They
go home.

6. Everett Fox, *In the Beginning: A New English Rendition of the Book
of Genesis* (New York: Schocken, 1983).

7. American television still assumed in the early 1960s that the typical
wife had promised to "love, honor, and obey" her husband at the marriage
ceremony. Wives were thought to regard this vow of obedience with a nuanced complexity that is hard to reconstruct in the black-and-white age we
live in. On the one hand it was a harmless joke; yet a husband who was unable (not often but occasionally) to command his own household was also a
joke. He seemed pitiful—especially to his wife.

8. Her achievements are named and praised, of course, in the abstract
or official or stereotyped language of the biblical poem; we don't list the real-
world achievements of the actual woman. Thus Jewish practice allows the
family to do a deed (heap praises on the lady of the house) that would otherwise be apt to overwhelm everyone (especially the lady herself) with self-
conscious embarrassment. Judaism is for human beings, not saints.

9. See, e.g., R. Mendel Shapiro, "*Qeri'at ha-Torah* by Women: A Halakhic Analysis," *Edah Journal* 1:2 (2001); R. Daniel Sperber, "Congregational
Dignity and Human Dignity: Women and Public Torah Reading," *Edah Journal* 3:2 (2002).

10. See, e.g., R. Gidon Rothstein, "Women's Aliyyot in Contemporary
Synagogues," *Tradition* 39:2 (2005).

11. It's only fair to note also some of the most consistently ignored dis-

sidents on the modern scene: women who feel no need to be propitiated by feminist change. As long ago as the 1970s, the great scholar and historian Lucy Dawidowicz wrote: "To my mind, the assumption by a woman of a rabbinic or priestly function in the synagogue undermines the very essence of Jewish tradition. To say that the 'Jewish women's movement' is inherently anti-traditionalist and implicitly antinomian is only to speak tautologically." "On Being a Woman in Shul," in Lucy Dawidowicz, *The Jewish Presence: Essays on Identity and History* (New York: Harcourt Brace Jovanovich, 1978, c1977).

12. The author knew what she was talking about. "By-the-bye," she writes in a letter to her sister Cassandra, "as I must leave off being young, I find many *douceurs* in being a sort of *chaperon*, for I am put on the sofa near the fire, and can drink as much wine as I like." As near as biographers can make out, her only love died before they had become engaged. Jane Austen never married, and died at 42.

13. Anthony Trollope, *Barchester Towers* (New York, 1857).

14. "Toward a Profile of the Tanna Akiba ben Joseph," *Journal of the American Oriental Society,* Volume 96 (1976).

## Chapter Five:
## Inward Pilgrimage

1. When the poet W. B. Yeats died in 1939, "he became his admirers," wrote the poet W. H. Auden (who was one of those admirers). "In the Grave I may speak through the stones," wrote the poet and preacher John Donne, "in the voice of my friends."

2. "Every word tells" is the foundation of Freudian psychoanalysis, too. By accident? Freud didn't believe in that kind of accident. He was reared in a Jewish household, and his father urged him to keep close to Judaism. Freud himself became an atheist, but his later work is increasingly obsessed with religion, especially Judaism.

3. In a sense this idea is foreshadowed at the start of Genesis. In the Bible, God brings each animal to Adam "to see what he would call them: and whatsoever Adam called every living creature, that was the name thereof" (2:18). Rémi Brague compares this account to the Koran's, in which God names every animal and teaches these names to Adam; "the idea according to which God could leave a region of liberty to man, wait for man's choice, and respect this choice, is thus [in the Koran's account] removed" (*Eccentric Culture: A Theory of Western Civilization* [South Bend, Indiana: St. Augustine's, 2002]).

4. Some readers have insisted that, all subtleties aside, Abraham behaved monstrously when he accepted God's command to kill his child. I believe they have missed an all-important fact about the story, which I will explain as we go along. Notwithstanding, it's obvious that in the remote past mankind (or large parts of it) believed that human sacrifice was necessary to propitiate the gods. Judaism would teach unequivocally that it was evil, and that paganism itself was evil. But Abraham was the first Jew. Despite his moral genius, he had lots to learn. It is wrong to condemn him because he didn't do what we would have done, given all that we and mankind have learned from Judaism, including from this very story.

5. The verse is cited in the New Testament; it was especially important to Puritans, whose idea of a "covenant community" depended in large part on this verse. The "covenant community" helped shape, in turn, the Puritan view of proto-American society.

6. A. J. Liebling, *Mollie and Other War Pieces* (New York: Ballantine, 1964).

7. Chesterton's introduction to Dickens's *Great Expectations* (New York: Dutton, 1950).

8. "Hope and the Absurd in the Work of Franz Kafka," in *The Myth of Sisyphus, and Other Essays* (New York: Knopf, 1955).

9. In a passage he deleted from *The Castle* (1926), cited by Max Brod in the Knopf edition (1948), translated by Edwin and Willa Muir. I return to Kafka below.

10. This explanation of Israelite circumcision has been proposed by others before, but has yet to be generally accepted.

11. I argued on similar lines that Jacob's struggle shows how "tense days explode into brightly colored nightmares" ("Tsipporah's Bloodgroom," *Orim* III:2 [Spring 1988]).

12. Graham Greene, *Our Man in Havana: An Entertainment* (London: Heinemann, 1958).

13. These thirteen principles have become part of the prayer book, enumerated verbatim in the daily morning service and recast as poetry in the hymn called *Yigdal*.

14. Meir Ben-Dov, *In the Shadow of the Temple: The Discovery of Ancient Jerusalem* (New York: Harper and Row, 1985).

15. Where does evil come from? What is it? After the flood, "the Lord said to Himself, I will undertake to curse the soil no more on man's account, for the urge of man's heart is evil from his youth" (Genesis 8:21). Evil is intrinsic to man's makeup. A midrash remarks that man could not survive without the "evil urge," which spurs him to build a home, marry, and earn a living. Yet, "sin crouches at the door; you are its desire, but you must over-

rule it" (Genesis 4:7). Man's duty is not to kill that urge but to keep it on a short leash.

Paul Kahn writes (*Out of Eden: Adam and Eve and the Problem of Evil* [Princeton, New Jersey: Princeton University Press, 2007]) that "Outside of fundamentalist religious groups, there is a reluctance to appeal to the idea of evil. . . . Evil is more than merely a point of view; it is not 'cured' by adopting new, more forgiving norms. . . . The sense of many people that modern philosophical discourses—particularly liberal theories—miss something essential is related to this failure to engage the problem of evil." These points have been made many times before but cannot be repeated too often. Most American conservatives agree with Kahn, whether or not they are part of "fundamentalist religious groups." But Kahn writes also that "the locus of evil" lies "in the refusal to recognize the possibility of one's own death," that "evil begins in the flight from death." These ideas seem (in general) indefensible. Some evil acts do seem like assertions of the evildoer's invulnerability; some evildoers do believe themselves to be immortal, or hope to be. But Kahn knows of such cases as (for example) Magda Goebbels, who arranged for the murder of her children in expectation of her own and her husband's imminent suicide; she had no illusions of immortality when she willed that her children die. Consider the two thugs hired to murder the Duke of Clarence in Shakespeare's *Richard III;* one suddenly becomes afraid—not to kill the Duke "but to be damn'd for killing him." The other reminds him of the reward Gloucester has promised once Clarence is dead, and that does the trick: "Zounds, he dies! I had forgot the reward." "Where's thy conscience now?" "O, in the Duke of Gloucester's purse." Shakespeare thus shows us a man who does evil in full awareness that he will die *and* be damned; he simply values the reward more than he fears the punishment. The idea that such people do evil to deny or abolish their own mortality rather than to get paid off *now* seems like a labored misreading of the psychology of evil.

16. The phrase is more compact and powerful in Hebrew.

17. The unclear evidence on the long-standing question of whether Brahms himself was of Jewish descent—among other points, an obvious derivation of "Brahms" seems to be from "Abrahmovitz" or a similar name—is discussed in Daniel Beller-McKenna, *Brahms and the German Spirit* (Cambridge, Massachusetts: Harvard University Press, 2004), especially 178–82. No conclusion is possible; more evidence is needed. So far, neither Gentile nor Jewish historians seem inclined to look for it.

18. Gentiles as well as Jews reach instinctively for the Psalms.

19. *Ribono shel olam, zo Torah v'zo s'kharah?* A young student who hears these colossal words in the original will never forget them. The same phrase is given to a different speaker in another Talmudic story.

20. *L'havdil:* I do not equate these two.

21. Everything we know about Jewish law and the Jewish community at the time of Jesus argues against the Gospel version of the Jews' role in his trial and death; see, among many other thorough treatments by Jews and non-Jews alike, Haim Cohn, *The Trial and Death of Jesus* (New York: Harper and Row, 1971). To say this implies no disrespect for Christianity. Even those modern Christians who are friendliest to Judaism maintain, as the logic of Christianity requires, that parts of the Hebrew Bible have been superseded by New Testament doctrine; and even those Jews friendliest to Christianity must reject certain narrative passages in the New Testament as untrue. If mutual respect is a suspension bridge, it requires two rock-steady foundations of self-respect to support the towers.

# Index